6/10/15. 5 QUESTIONS

① WHY AM [I]
ALIVE [?]

② WHY DO I DO WHAT I DO?
EVERY PERSON ON THE PLANET
HAS A CALLING, WHICH, POINTS
THE HEART TO WHAT IS RIGHT.

③ WHY DO I HAVE WHAT I HAVE?
CONSIDER THE NEEDS OF
OTHERS WHO ARE DESPERATE
FOR HELP.

④ WHO IS GOING WITH ME?
IN THE MOST DESPERATE TIMES
OF OUR LIVES, WE NEED FRIENDS
WHO WILL WALK WITH US IN THE
DARKNESS. WE NEED FRIENDS
IN THE GOOD TIMES, TOO.

⑤ WHAT AM I CARRYING ON THE
JOURNEY?
THE DECISION TO TRAVEL LIGHT IS
CRUCIAL IF WE WANT TO GET WHERE
WE WANT TO GO.

Five Questions, Two Perspectives,
and the Pursuit of Purpose

THE LEPERS'
LESSONS

KEVIN PAUL SCOTT
PAULUS WIRATNO

Cover design and interior formatting by Anne McLaughlin, Blue Lake Design,
Dickinson, Texas
ISBN: 978-0-9907879-0-7
Published by Baxter Press, Friendswood, Texas
First printing 2015
Printed in the United States

What people are saying about *The Lepers' Lessons* . . .

"Stories capture our imaginations and take us places we've never dreamed of going. The very best stories not only entertain us; they inspire us to do more and be more. In this book, Kevin and Paulus take us into a scene in the ancient past to teach us the most important lessons for today. Read this book. You'll never be the same."

—*Mark Batterson, Lead Pastor of National Community Church in Washington, DC and Author of the Bestseller,* The Circle Maker, *and* The Grave Robber

"In this book, Kevin Paul Scott delivers a powerful message packed with insight and inspiration. This biblical story comes to life in a fresh way as Scott and Wiratno encourage readers to discover significance in their lives. *The Lepers' Lessons* is Chuck Norris approved!"

—*Chuck Norris, Actor, Film Producer, Screenwriter, and Expert in Martial Arts*

"I have observed Kevin inspire individuals for many years, but this may be his best work. Who knew that the answer to five simple questions could stimulate the imagination, capture the heart, and provide clear direction for the future? In *The Lepers' Lessons*, Kevin Scott and Paulus Wiratno accomplish all three of these important goals. They have proven to be perceptive students of human nature and leaders who can point people to a meaningful tomorrow."

—*Vince Dooley, former Head Football Coach and Athletic Director for the University of Georgia*

"Leaders are shaped more by challenges than by successes. It's in the dark times that the light of hope and purpose shines most brightly. This is the story of Paulus Wiratno, a valuable partner with my ministry, Leading the Way. In *The Lepers' Lessons*, Paulus and his co-author Kevin Paul Scott ask some of the best questions anyone can consider. Our answers shape our future and determine our impact on others . . . for the rest of our lives."

—*Dr. Michael Youssef, Founder and President of Leading the Way, Author of* The Leadership Style of Jesus

"Kevin Scott and Paulus Wiratno take ancient principles and launch them into the 21st century. Their interesting insights regarding the lepers of old position them as transformational agents of relevant truth. Clarity, compassion, and dedication are central to every leadership book Kevin Scott writes."

—*Dr. John D Hull , CEO of Crossroads Global Media Group*

"Kevin Paul Scott and Paulus Wiratno have penned a book that will stand the test of time as long as humans inhabit the planet. The authors delve into questions mankind has been asking since the beginning of time and we find ourselves asking daily. This book will provide solace for those who seek answers to some of life's most perplexing and profound questions. I am glad to see these authors enter into the literary fray."

—*Mitch Albom, New York Times Bestselling Author of* Tuesdays with Morrie

"*The Lepers' Lessons* is a must-read book. It addresses the questions we all ask ourselves in our life's journey from why are we alive to what now. In uncertain times such as these, with wars and economic crises, we find ourselves asking these crucial questions. The authors provide answers and help the reader establish personal order in their lives. Highly recommended!"

—*Megyn Kelly, Host of "The Kelly File" on Fox News Channel*

"The Lepers' Lessons is a powerful message that addresses many of life's profound questions in a way that will invigorate readers. This book reminds us that we were made by God and for God, and we'll find God's answers if we stay with Him on the journey. Scott and Wiratno have written a book that will stand the test of time."

—*Rick Warren, Pastor of Saddleback Church and Bestselling Author of* The Purpose-Driven Life

"A powerful story, beautifully told. *The Lepers' Lessons* surprised me. I hadn't expected to get so much contemporary, practical help from an ancient story. Kevin and Paulus have a firm handle on what gives life meaning, and they're generous to share their insights with us in this book."

—*Rodney Bullard, Executive Director of the Chick-fil-A Foundation and Vice President of Community Affairs, Chick-fil-A, Inc.*

"Every great story has a surprise or two that keeps you on the edge of your seat. *The Lepers' Lessons*, however, is far better than just a novel. It's an actual historical account that helps us uncover the most important lessons for today! I recommend this awesome book to anyone who is hungry for some timeless principles that lead to a more satisfying life!"

—*Mike Linch, Senior Pastor at NorthStar Church, Kennesaw, Georgia*

"Paulus and Marlieyse are two of the greatest leaders I know. They are the real deal. Living and serving Jesus in the largest Muslim nation on earth with an amazing strategy for winning Indonesia for Jesus, they are unstoppable. These two people are filled with courage, vision, passion and compassion. What's happening in their ministry is truly amazing. I know this book will bless you and encourage you."

—*Jack Hanes, Senior Pastor of Imagine Nations Church, Former Missions Director for the Assemblies of God, ACC, in Australia*

"When we make our journey in life, we arrive at crucial junctures that become our defining moments. We can see some of them approaching, but others seem to burst forth from nowhere. Our responses to these defining moments shape our future and our legacy. In *The Lepers' Lessons*, Kevin and Paulus encourage us to be brutally honest about our opportunities and challenges—and face them with courage, faith, and hope. When we do, then and only then, can we live the life God intended for us to live!"

—*Dr. Dwight "Ike" Reighard, Senior Pastor of Piedmont Church, Marietta, Georgia, and CEO of MUST Ministries*

"I've had the distinct privilege of knowing Paulus Wiratno for years. I've seen how his clear, insightful, and powerful message of hope inspires people to be more and do more, and I've seen how his compassion has given many children a future they never dreamed possible. This book by Paulus and his partner Kevin Scott asks—and answers—the most important questions in our lives. I am happy to recommend this book to anyone who wants to make a difference. It will change your life."

—*Horst Schultze, Former President of Ritz Carlton, Current Chairman and C.E.O. of The Capella Hotel Group*

Kevin . . .

To Andy and Carolyn Smith, my adopted grandparents, for being examples of the message of this book: living for a higher purpose and having a profound impact on my life.

Paulus . . .

To Marliesye, my loving companion and best friend.

To Debora, Irene and Timothy, our three children, who have amazingly enriched my life.

To Mercy Children all over Indonesia, who have given me a sense of fulfillment.

CONTENTS

AN UNLIKELY CONNECTION

Before you dive into this book, the authors want to give you some background about how we met and why we decided to work together on this project.

From Kevin . . .

For several years I helped lead a company that took American students on study abroad programs to countries around the world. Our purpose was to show them different cultures, expose them to needs and opportunities, and equip them to serve at home and abroad. At one point, another program asked my business partner, Garrett Gravesen, and me to travel and speak at their events. It was the best of all possible worlds: Garrett and I got to talk to students about making their lives count, but we didn't have to make the elaborate, complex, and always-changing travel plans.

The organization asked us to join some students in Australia, accompany them on a tour of the Great Barrier Reef, and finally, on to New Zealand. Garrett, who is always thinking of how to do things more creatively, checked to see if we could leave a week early and travel through Singapore on our way to Sydney. We wanted a weeklong layover in Indonesia on the island of Bali, which is a short plane flight from Singapore. When he told me about his idea, it sounded both absurd and wonderful—and best of all, it worked out.

I had traveled all over the world with our study abroad program, but never on a vacation. International trips sound glamorous, but there is little time for fun when you're the one responsible for dozens of college students, schedules, exchanging money, paying bills, keeping people from getting exotic viruses, and caring for the ones who inevitably get sick. On this trip to Bali, Garrett and I planned to take the entire week off. We were going to paradise to relax, drink coffee, ride an elephant, go to the Monkey Forest, and eat foods we had never even heard of before.

The day we left Atlanta, I posted on Facebook: "Headed out on an adventure. Going to Bali!" A friend, Jonathan Youssef, immediately replied, "When you're in Bali, I want you to meet my friend, Paulus Wiratno. You'll be amazed."

I thought, *Why not? If he's Jonathan's friend, maybe it'll be fun to look him up.*

Garrett and I arrived in Bali on a Friday, and I called Paulus. He didn't know me at all, except that Jonathan Youssef was my friend. Without a moment of hesitation, Paulus invited me to speak at his church on Sunday.

That morning we arrived at an orphanage that also serves as a church. I don't remember what I told the people there. In my jet-lagged brain, I'm not sure I even knew what I was saying as I spoke, but the people were very kind and listened attentively. After church,

Garrett and I got to spend time with Paulus and his wife Marliesye and hear their incredible story of survival, faith, and compassion.

We had planned to relax all week, but instead, I discovered that Paulus was a man with a compelling sense of purpose who inspires others to get involved in what he is doing. Don't get me wrong. Paulus doesn't live at a frantic pace with his teeth clenched in intensity. He has a huge vision to have an impact on people, but he blends it with a calm, peaceful certainty that God is always in control. He's an amazing man. As he told us his life's story, I hung on every word. During that amazing week, my heart was deeply moved. It still is.

Our time with Paulus not only changed the trajectory of our week; it changed the trajectory of my life. Before meeting him, I had measured effectiveness primarily by the visible standards of success: the number of people involved and the amount of money changing hands. Just listening to his story challenged me to evaluate my life, my direction, and my reasons for doing what I do each day. Paulus inspired me to dream bigger and do more—to influence more people with a more expansive vision.

A few months later, Paulus came to America to meet with individuals and engage donors in the work he was doing in Indonesia. I asked him to come to Atlanta, and I had him tell his story to every group I could gather: the staff in our organization, a men's Bible study, our church, other leaders in the city, and my family. I wanted them to be as inspired and challenged as I had been— and they were. In every location and to each audience, his message was the same—your life can be significant! Paulus repeatedly used an ancient story of four lepers as an illustration to speak to each individual's quest for self-worth and the opportunity to make an impact.

But there's a problem: I can't take Paulus with me across the country and around the world. My solution is this book—a platform where I can share his message with everyone everywhere. This message—the concepts, principles, and applications—are life changing. I've internalized them and applied them to my life. At each opportunity I share them with the people in the organization I lead and to the businesses and groups with whom I speak. But even that world is too small. The principles apply to every person: young and old; the popular and the overlooked; the up-and-comers and the down-and-outers; Asians, Americans, Europeans; Hindus, Buddhists, Muslims, Jews, and Christians. Paulus and I both have a distinctly Christian perspective, but the concepts in this book are universal.

After meeting Paulus for the first time in Bali, I finished my trip to Australia and New Zealand. When I flew back to America, I found it too easy to slip back into my old routine: I had a business to build, friends to see, and meetings to attend. I continued to feel the pressures to be successful, manage events, and drive dollars to the bottom line. But a dozen times each day, I kept hearing Paulus's voice asking me the five questions we had discussed when we met. The questions—and the answers that they demanded—reframed everything I was doing.

I've found it to be the same with others who hear these lessons. It doesn't happen immediately, and it certainly doesn't happen easily, but it happens. For me, the answer to these questions was not to sell everything and move to Indonesia. In fact, I'm still doing many of the same things I had been doing before, but I'm acting with a depth of insight and a richer, purer purpose than I had ever experienced. It has made a difference . . . a big difference . . . in my most important relationships, my work, and every other aspect of life. I'll never be the same.

Paulus's life has changed mine, and this story has the inherent power to change the lives of anyone who is open to listen and consider the profound implications. I hope you're one of those people.

From Paulus . . .

In 1998 I lived with my family in a refugee camp on Ambon Island in Indonesia. My wife Marliesye and I had two daughters. Debbie was ten years old, and Irene was only four. A war between Muslim jihadists and Christians had torn the community apart. For centuries, Ambon had been predominantly Muslim, but in the past few decades many people had become believers in Jesus Christ. Now the Muslims wanted the island back. They started with threats, but when verbal intimidation didn't work Muslim extremists escalated their efforts by burning churches, martyring pastors, and slaughtering many Christians.

Before the war started, we had a church and a Bible school. Both were destroyed, and two of our students were killed. We were forced to flee to a refugee camp—the only safe place on the island. It was a dismal existence as more than 15,000 people crowded into far too insufficient accommodations. We slept on the bare dirt in tents (in a school building). Marliesye and I had to stand in line four hours each day to receive a little rice to sustain our family. Disease and starvation stalked every person in the camp. We saw people die every day. A few yards outside the gate, jihadists were waiting for anyone brave enough or foolish enough to leave. The war wasn't over. Every day we heard gunshots and explosions just outside the fence. Every time a bomb exploded, my daughter Irene was traumatized and gasped for breath. We lived on a razor's edge between life and death.

For months we tried to hold together our family and the remnants of our displaced community, but conditions continued to deteriorate. I felt we had to get out of the camp so we could survive, but we had no resources and nowhere to go. Marliesye and I had moved 23 times before we went to Ambon to pastor the church and lead the Bible school. We didn't want to move again, but it was clear that a war zone was no place to raise our daughters. A friend from Australia, Rod Plummer, called me with advice and a gracious offer: "Paulus, I know you love Ambon, but you need to move your family to Bali. You'll be safe, and you can start over there." Bali, Rod knew, is predominantly Hindu, so it would be a peaceful respite from the war-plagued environment where we had been staying.

Rod's church gave us $2000 so we could move to Bali, and he put us up in a hotel for two weeks after we got there. It was a glorious relief, but our eyes were on the future, not the past or the present. After a week or so in Bali, Rod asked, "Paulus, what are you going to do on this island? What will be your work, your ministry, your calling?"

I didn't know. At the moment I was just glad that the four of us were alive and that Irene could breathe. Still, I knew God had something for us to do. I was ready for him to turn to a new page in the story of our lives. Rod invited me to attend a pastors' conference at his church in Towoomba City, Australia. During the event, a man named Jack Hanes spoke on an often-overlooked passage in 2 Kings in the Old Testament. Jack's explanation of the story and his applications, though, were as fresh as that morning's sunrise. It was as if I were the only person sitting in the audience. God was speaking directly through Jack to my heart.

That day Jack drew several piercing questions out of the story of four lepers who had been on the brink of starvation and death, and my life began a new transition. A hundred questions had been swirling in my mind since the day the extremists burned our school and forced our family to flee to the refugee camp. Even moving to Bali and finding some peace and relief hadn't answered all my questions. Suddenly I realized I didn't have a hundred questions; I had only a few—the ones Jack was asking—that would determine the direction of the rest of my life. Those piercing questions clarified my purpose, my marriage, my relationships with my children, and the work I would pursue for the rest of my career.

The first question Jack asked when he told the story of the lepers was, "Why am I still alive?" That wasn't an academic or hypothetical question to me. In the war on Ambon, two of my students had been killed and more than 2,000 other Christians had been murdered. While in the camp I held a one-year-old baby who died in my arms. Every day Irene struggled to breathe when the concussion of explosions rocked the camp. I wondered if each breath would be her last. When Jack asked the question at the pastors' conference, it couldn't have been more relevant. I had to answer it. Why, in fact, was I still alive when death had been all around me? Why had I been spared? What could I do with the rest of my life that would be ultimately meaningful? I couldn't make sense of the many acts of hatred and violence, but choosing to live with love, kindness, wisdom, and strength would at least begin to overcome the evil we had suffered.

The questions that were born from Jack Hanes's message have become my life's message. The answers to those questions have shaped who I am, what I say, and what I do. I talk about them to individuals and congregations, to people of all faiths, and in every country where I travel.

When I met with the mayor of a large city in Australia, we talked about these questions. He asked, "I know my life is short, and I want it to count. Paulus, will you help me?"

Victor, a successful businessman, flew to Bali to meet with me because someone had told him about the questions. He sat in my office in his finely tailored suit and sadly explained, "Help me, Pastor Paulus. I have everything money can buy, but my life is empty."

Kylie is a young woman with a heart for others, but she wasn't sure how to invest her life. After she heard the five questions and wrestled with the answers, she found a new, exciting direction and determined to devote her life to care for hurting people.

Currently our organization runs twelve orphanages in Indonesia. The children who come to us are broken, alone, and hopeless. The questions that have changed the lives of mayors, business leaders, and middle-class people are the same questions that give orphans a clear vision that their lives can count.

It may sound as if I'm saying the questions have some kind of magic powers. They don't. They simply probe beneath the surface of every person's life to uncover purpose, motivation, and power. They make decisions clearer for anyone who has the courage to answer them.

Not everyone has such courage. I received an invitation to travel to Australia to speak to a group of twenty leaders. A limousine picked me up at the airport and took me to a fine hotel. Later that day in their corporate offices, I poured my heart out to them, told the story of the lepers, and asked the questions that have changed so many lives, but the executives were bored. As far as I could tell, nothing happened in anyone's life that day. Not everyone wants to be challenged. Not everyone is open to being changed. Maybe they will remember the questions when they're more open. I hope so.

I've found that most people have an instinctive desire to find out how they can make a difference. They want their lives to count, and they feel a measure of frustration because something (they usually aren't sure what) is missing. It is my great joy and privilege to step into their lives to help them find the buried treasure of a meaningful future. It has become the desire of my life to connect those who long to do something meaningful with others who are caring for people with mercy, love, and truth.

Our Hope for You

We suspect that some people have picked up this book because it's their last attempt to find meaning in their lives. They've gone to conferences, read books, attended self-help seminars, and sought answers, but they still feel empty. In fact, because they've looked so hard for so long, they feel ashamed that they haven't found "it" yet. They hope the message of this book holds the answers they've been looking for.

Others appear to have it all together. They have fine clothes, a nice car, a beautiful place to live, wonderful vacations, and plenty of money, but they lack the one thing they really want: fulfillment. They hope this book will cut through the false promises of their culture and help them discover real meaning.

Still others are just trying to survive each day. They may not live in refugee camps and face disease and starvation, but they may face the chronic pain of living with past failures that haunt their memories. Maybe they have patterns of destructive behaviors that hinder progress, or perhaps they relate to demanding people who consume their joy and energy. Whatever they face, they hope this book will give them new hope and direction.

I (Paulus) regularly visit a refugee camp in East Timor that serves as home for 47,000 people who have fled the same kind of civil war I experienced on Ambon Island years ago. When I walk through the camp, children grab both of my hands and beg me, "Please, Pastor Paulus, take me to Mercy Home! I want to go to school!" I'm instantly in tears because we can't take them all. But when I speak at churches and in businesses around the world, eager people figuratively take my hands and ask, "Please, Pastor Paulus, show me how I can make a difference! I want my life to count!" Inherently, they realize that someday they're going to die, and they want the world to be a better place when they leave it than when they were born—if not on a global scale, at least in their families, their neighborhoods, and in the lives of the people they work with each day.

I'm called to play a tiny role in God's grand design. I make connections between people and God, people and their dreams, people and their own resources, and people and the crying needs of the unfortunate in the world. It is my great joy to see God use me in these ways.

Each of us has a desire to live for a purpose far bigger than ourselves, whether we happen to be an orphan in a refugee camp, a middle class mother or father, or the wealthiest person in the city. We hope our message in this book rekindles your hope, stirs your imagination, challenges your current status, and inspires you to live a life of true significance.

Nothing less will do.

Authors' notes:

When books are co-authored, it's important to note the person who is telling a particular story or relating a specific principle. In this book, we will indicate the speaker in parentheses when it's necessary.

In the Appendix you will find questions related to each chapter that are designed to stimulate personal reflection and group discussion. Don't hurry through those. Take time to think, pray, and consider each point so the questions—and the answers to the questions—will sink deep into your heart, your attitude, and your actions. The first set of questions relates to Chapter 1.

THE STORY

The total collapse of society.

A military catastrophe.

Human nature pushed to the breaking point . . . and beyond.

Words on a page can't convey the gnawing sense of hopelessness and utter misery of people suffering from famine in a city besieged by a foreign power.

Centuries ago, the Israelites living in Samaria were attacked by the king of Syria, and his powerful army surrounded the city. As days and weeks passed, food supplies dwindled to nothing. In desperation they resorted to eating the last of the donkeys . . . and then the scraps of meat on the donkey's head. The situation was grim. Every person in the city was dying of starvation—a slow, agonizing death.

Another group of people, however, were in even worse distress. Every community had a leper colony outside the city walls. According to Israel's laws and customs, lepers were considered "unclean." They had to live apart from their families and friends, and they weren't permitted to interact with healthy people in the cities. They were already outcasts, and now they also suffered from starvation and increased exposure to military attack. At that moment, the lepers were the most vulnerable people in Samaria.

On the brink of extinction, four lepers sat together outside the city gates. They considered their situation with candor and courage. They told each other: "Everyone in the city is starving, and the Syrians are about to attack. If we stay here at the gates, we'll die."

One suggested they try to get into the city behind the walls, but another remarked, "What good is that? If we go in there, we'll starve and die."

"We can't just sit here," said another. "We'll die if we do nothing!"

One of them had a radical idea: "Let's go to the army of the Syrians and surrender ourselves to them. If they give us food and spare our lives, we'll live. If they have no mercy, we'll die."

They looked at one another and almost laughed at the absurdity of the idea: four lepers approaching a bloodthirsty enemy for help. Finally, one of them said, "Hey, we have nothing to lose."

As the sun was going down over the city and the shadows grew longer, the four men hobbled down a dusty trail. They must have been a sight. Leprosy literally makes the body numb to pain. The flesh doesn't rot away; instead, the lack of pain causes lepers to be injured and reinjured without even noticing. The wounds get so bad that body parts become infected and fall off. They may have been missing fingers, toes, noses, or ears. They wore rags and shuffled along on bare feet. The stench must have been unbearable to anyone within a hundred feet of them—except other lepers who had become used to the smell.

As they walked a mile or so to the enemy camp, darkness fell across the land. And although they didn't realize it, a miracle was occurring. The Syrian soldiers heard a distant rumbling sound grow louder . . . and then deafening . . . like the approach of a tornado. To their ears, it was the threatening sound of hundreds of chariots and the march of a mighty army! The soldiers, so confident and fierce just moments before, became terrified. They assumed Israel's king had hired other armies to attack them, and they ran away in fear of their lives! They left everything behind: gold, silver, clothes, horses, donkeys, and equipment. It was as if the muffled crunching sound of each leper's footsteps had been magnified a million times, and an entire army had fled in panic by the time the four lepers arrived.

Meanwhile, unaware of the chaos in the Syrian camp, the lepers were probably rehearsing the desperate plea they would make to the first soldiers when they arrived. They only had one chance to ask for mercy, so it had better be a good speech! As they reached the outskirts of the camp, they walked up to the first tent. To their shock, it was empty. They quickly looked around to see if anyone was watching them. No one was around. No one at all.

On a blanket on the floor of the tent was a huge dinner spread in front of them. The soldiers had left behind a banquet! The four lepers ate and drank more and better food than they had ever tasted. They hadn't been full since . . . well, they couldn't remember when they had eaten enough to fill their stomachs. During the meal, they looked around at all the things in the tent. Much was carefully stored, but some had been thrown away as the soldiers fled only moments before the men arrived. The four lepers grabbed as much stuff as they could carry and ran into the bushes to hide it all.

One of them asked, "Did you see any soldiers?"

The others shook their heads. One replied, "Are you thinking what I'm thinking?"

They ran to the next tent and found it full of riches. They hurriedly picked up all they could carry and again ran into the bushes to hide their loot.

They realized they could keep hiding their treasures for days, but then one of them had a very different idea: "Hey, what are we thinking? This is wrong. This is a day not only for us, but our whole nation. We're treating it like it's our own party! Let's go back to the city to tell everyone else the good news!" The others agreed.

We can only imagine all the thoughts that filled their minds on their walk back to the city. They had left with a slim hope of survival for themselves; now they returned with incredible news that would save everyone. They had rehearsed their speech to ask for mercy. Now they rehearsed their proclamation of glorious rescue!

By the time they reached the city gates, it was pitch dark. They called to the sentry on the city walls, "You won't believe this, but we went to the enemy camp and it was deserted. Completely deserted, except that they have left everything behind. Food, clothes, horses, gold . . . everything! We're saved, I tell you. We're saved!"

The sentry rushed the report to the king, who immediately sent scouts to investigate. They came back with verification: "The story is true! In fact, we found clothes and equipment thrown away by the Syrians all along the road to the Jordan River!"

Teams went out to gather all the food to bring back to the starving people of the city. They also picked up other riches the Syrians had left behind. The city had been saved by a most unlikely group of people: four lepers—outcasts and seemingly helpless, but willing to take a desperate step and see what might happen.

Five Questions

When the story begins, the four lepers have three choices, none of which looks very promising: If they stay outside the city walls, they'll surely die. If they go inside where people are dying from the famine, they'll certainly die. The only option left is for them to throw themselves on the mercy of an army that has shown no mercy. If they go to the Syrians, they'll probably die, but it's their only hope.

Walking to the camp must have been excruciating—physically, mentally, and psychologically. They had been almost immobilized by their disease, and now they had to walk in the last light of day down a dirt road. Every pebble was an obstacle. When they arrived, they fully expected to be executed, but instead they were stunned to discover they were suddenly rich beyond their wildest dreams! The initial human response of greed was evident, but it was soon replaced with a more altruistic vision for the future. Their news could rescue everyone—including those who had mocked them and avoided them because of their disease. "All we have received," they realized, "isn't for us, but for others."

They instinctively asked five questions that are as relevant for us today as they were for them:

1) "Why am I still alive?"

By every reasonable expectation, the four men should have been dead, but they were spared. Their first instinct was survival—eating and drinking to stave off starvation—but they soon realized they were alive for a bigger purpose.

2) "Why do I do what I do?"

What began as a desperate act to save themselves transformed into an opportunity to save their nation. One of the lepers had a sudden insight: he was alive to do something to help others. When he suggested sharing their newfound blessings with the entire camp, his companions immediately approved his plan. Every person on the planet has a calling, which, like a compass points north, points the heart to what is right. Though the lepers had been dying only moments before, they knew the right thing to do. Compassion overcame greed; love surpassed fear. A new motivation gripped them, changed them, and empowered them.

3) "Why do I have what I have?"

The men suddenly had more resources than they needed to live another day. They could hoard, or they could give—a choice that was unimaginable only minutes earlier. They could be completely self-absorbed, or they could consider the needs of others who were desperate for help. The abundance of their riches, they understood, could do far more than make their lives a little more comfortable. It could change the future of individuals, families, and a nation.

4) "Who is going with me?"

These four men had suffered together for years, and heartache had surely brought them closer together. During the siege, they faced starvation together, and the shared anguish made them even closer. When they took the radical, crazy risk to ask the enemy to save them, they went together.

In the most desperate times of our lives, we need friends who walk with us in the darkness. We need friends in the good times, too. In times of the greatest opportunity, we need people who will encourage us, prod us to dream even bigger dreams, and celebrate with us. It took only one of the four to suggest saving the city instead of keeping everything for themselves, but the others loved and trusted him so much that they all agreed to return immediately—with empty hands but full hearts. We can almost see the huge smiles on their faces as they shuffled hurriedly back to Samaria to shout the good news of deliverance. If one fell, another picked him up. Together they faced death, and together they brought life.

We all need friends like that.

5) "What am I carrying on the journey?"

If the four men had tried to carry armloads of riches back to the city, they wouldn't have made it. They could barely walk when their hands were empty; they certainly couldn't carry loads of loot on a long night hike over a rough road. They had to make hard decisions about what to carry, and they realized carrying good news was more valuable than carrying stuff—no matter how valuable it might have seemed when they first acquired it. A little insight, some compassion, and a measure of courage enabled them to lighten their load so they could arrive at their destination.

Many people carry heavy loads of guilt, bitterness, anxiety, and memories of past failures. Such burdens weigh them down as they try to make their way in life. They don't enjoy the journey, and they don't arrive at their destination. The decision to travel light is crucial if we want to get where we want to go.

Imagine

In the best novels and movies, we get swept up in the story. We feel what the protagonist feels. We take on the hopes and fears of the character. We can see ourselves in the place of the actors. That's how we want you to think of this story.

Put yourself in the lepers' place from beginning to end. Capture a sense of their desperation as they contemplate death. It isn't just that they have lost hope in the moment; they have lived as despised outcasts all their lives! What are they talking about as they walk into the rising darkness toward the Syrian camp? As they approach the first tent, hear them gasp and sigh because they might have only seconds to live. Are you there with them? Do you sense the intensity of both desperate hope and mortal fear?

Every great story has a plot twist. This one has two. First, the men are shocked that no one is in the first tent, and even more so to discover the bounty of goods left for them to take. The men gorged on delicious food, better than they had ever tasted. Then they grabbed all they could carry to hide so they would be secure for the rest of their lives. They found the pirates' treasure, but it wasn't hidden at all!

The second plot twist took place after they hid the goods from the second tent, when one of them had a pang of conscience like a lightning bolt on a dark night. He realized they had a chance to do something noble. The act was so loving, so self-sacrificing, and so powerful that they all immediately agreed to live for a cause far more worthwhile than their own comfort.

Then imagine being one of the group on the dirt road back to the city. Would you have had second thoughts? Do you suppose a couple of them tried to figure out how to get back to the things they had hidden before anyone else could find them? There's no record of such doubts. All we can be sure of is that the joy of helping other desperate people surpassed their fear of returning to a destitute condition as outcasts beyond the gates.

Now envision the scene at the gates. Did the sentry have a hard time hearing what they were saying because they all were yelling at the same time? They had to have been as excited as fans seeing the winning shot taken at the last second. But they got their message across.

And then imagine the hours, days, weeks, and years that followed. Those men were still lepers—they still smelled like rotten fish and looked like characters on *The Walking Dead*—but they were heroes to the entire community. Even if others occasionally forgot how they had saved the nation, the four friends never forgot that day. They had gone from the bottom of their society to the very top.

If we learn to see life through their eyes, through the lenses of these five questions, we can unlock the desires of our hearts and unleash our potential to achieve them. These five questions move us from the mundane to the meaningful. Discovering a new, compelling sense of purpose doesn't mean that you have to walk away from everything you're doing. While it may require some drastic changes, most of what you're doing will probably remain the same. In any case, your answers to the five questions will infuse more meaning into your life than ever before.

Different Points in Life, Different Questions

For the lepers, all five questions were compressed into a single experience. For most of us, however, it doesn't work that way. At different times in our lives, we face particular obstacles or opportunities that force us (or invite us) to ask one or two specific questions.

The big existential question, "Why do I exist?" is the same as "Why am I still alive?" We naturally ask this question at major turning points in our lives:

- graduation from high school or college;

- choosing a career;

- on our wedding day;

- when the person we loved marries someone else;

- when we get a dreaded phone call;

- when we get a promotion;

- when someone else gets the job;

- at the birth of a child;

- as we sit at a funeral; or

- at middle age when our youthful idealism often crashes into a stubborn reality.

For some people the question of purpose (#1) is crystal clear. They have a goal in business, a political cause, or a service project they love. Their biggest issue is uncovering the driving force that propels their actions.

The question of motivation (#2) can arise at any moment, often when we realize we've been too self-absorbed, using people and loving things instead of loving people and using things for a higher purpose.

The question about resources (#3) isn't just for the rich and powerful. Each of us has incredible resources of time and talents to invest in meaningful activities, and many of us have far more money and possessions than we really need. The lure of advertising is that we can never have enough, that we always need to buy the next product or service. Actually, the ads are true in a sense: no amount of "things" can ever provide ultimate fulfillment. We need more than they can offer. Our possessions only fill shelves, not hearts. Most people buy things they don't need with money they don't have to impress people they don't like.

We may need to ask the question about friendships (#4) more often. Our companions greatly influence our destination, but it's easy to drift along with the people who make us feel comfortable. We need at least a few devoted friends who challenge us to reach higher and who have the guts to tell us the truth—the hard truths that we really don't want to hear.

As for Question #5, most of us carry the dead weight of emotional baggage far too long. We become used to it, so the load feels completely normal. The excess baggage can even serve as a useful excuse for why we haven't made more progress toward our goal, and we may use it to convince ourselves there's no use in having any goal at all. Paradoxically, painful baggage can become a source of false comfort.

But there's another paradox: we often learn life's most important lessons in times of stress, loss, and suffering. Heartaches are watershed moments. When we face them, we either become wiser, more compassionate, and more humble, or we become hardened, resentful, and full of self-pity because our lives didn't go the way we planned.

Before the siege and the famine, the lepers lived a meaningless, routine existence. Facing death forced them to make an incredibly difficult decision. Then, sudden wealth enabled them to make another extraordinary decision. They would have never had the opportunity to be courageous and compassionate if they hadn't looked death in the face.

The hardest times in our lives are our greatest teachers. They are open doors, inviting us to walk into a new future. They appear terribly threatening, and we would rather run or fight than walk through them, but they steer us toward opportunities to grow in wisdom, kindness, and strength. They may even be the passageways to our true calling.

That's what happened to me (Paulus) when my family was stuck in the Indonesian refugee camp. We had been serving God and enjoying our lives together, but the war on Ambon Island took everything from us. I've heard it said that when God closes a door he opens another one, but sometimes he takes a long time to open it! For months, our situation appeared completely hopeless. Our grand vision of the future shrank to the immediate essentials of getting enough rice to survive another day, not contracting dysentery, and making sure Irene was still breathing whenever we heard the explosions. During those days, I wasn't making grand plans to be effective. I simply wondered if we would live.

The hardest times in life are disguised opportunities. If we find enough courage to keep going, they become magnificent turning points. Our heartaches become the platform for our greatest impact for the rest of our lives.

The Consultant's Strategy

In my (Kevin's) speaking to organizations and consulting with leaders, people often ask a variation of the questions, "How can I find purpose for my life?" And, "How can I figure out how my life can really matter?" The people who ask aren't limited to a single bracket of age, vocation, or income. They are top executives and single moms, people near retirement and those who are just starting out, those who look like they have all the answers and those whose lives are wrecked. Every person on the planet has an inherent drive to live a life that makes a difference.

The best coaches and consultants don't come in with a notebook full of slick answers. Instead, they come with a few piercing questions. The most effective leadership and organizational consultants know the conversation isn't about their wisdom, insights, and experience; it's about uncovering the hidden wisdom, insights, and experiences of the person asking for help.

The five questions the lepers intuitively asked are the very best questions a consultant could ask a client—no matter the client's age, gender, class, or condition. The struggle to answer the questions paves the path to a life of significance. I'm not overstating the proposition; I believe it with all my heart. I've seen these questions bring light into dark corners of a person's life, and I've seen them clarify the direction and motivations of a person's heart . . . including mine. The first question identifies and affirms a person's purpose in life, and the others shape the motivation and provide steps required to fulfill it.

Many people are so absorbed in their daily lives that they don't even ask the most fundamental question. They are so busy dealing with the pressure to perform, the desire to win approval, the game of not being left behind, and the lure of filling their lives with pleasure that they never get around to asking, "Why am I still alive?" And if they hear others asking that question, they may feel threatened because they realize a good answer will require change, and they're not sure what the change will cost them. Would having a new sense of purpose change their relationships? Would it alter their career path? Or worse, would it make them weird?

We may begin asking questions for many different reasons. A crisis naturally forces us to ask hard questions to try to make sense of life. Something that takes us out of our comfort zones, like international travel, enables us to see things from a different perspective and may begin the questioning. A stab of conscience—a sense of guilt because we've done something foolish—can propel us into productive self-examination. And hearing the stories of wise and brave people inspires us to ask, "They did something important and worthwhile. What about me?"

Most of us will need to go back to the fundamental questions many times in our lives. Ours is a plugged-in generation that's always listening, always watching, always connecting. On any day, we confront a thousand distractions—not necessarily evil things because even good things can totally absorb our time, our minds, and our hearts. But when we get so busy, we desperately need to create some space to reflect.

Forces in our society are conspiring to prevent us from asking important questions. A few years ago a *Newsweek* article cited a study showing that preschool children ask their parents an average of 100 questions every day. But by middle school, they have essentially stopped asking questions. The article notes that in early adolescence, student motivation and engagement in activities often falls sharply. Eventually, it affects all of us.

Are we too entertained? Too bored? Do we stop asking questions because we've lost interest, or do we lose interest because the system (pervasive entertainment, plugged-in generation) doesn't stimulate us to keep asking important questions?

It's never too late to start asking great questions again. The answers may not come quickly, but stay with it. Keep asking until you arrive at meaningful answers.

The five questions are an effective template to focus our thoughts and take us deeper into real reflection—and we need to think often about them. At various points we need correction, and at other times we need confirmation of why we're doing what we're doing. Our motivations can drift to competition instead of compassion, so we may need to evaluate the impact our friends are having on us (and the impact we're having on them). We need to continually evaluate our direction and our destination, making sure to unload the unhealthy baggage that weighs us down. The lepers' questions are evaluation tools, but they're more than that. They give us hope that the answers will always open new doors of fresh meaning, renewed joy, deeper love, and more effectiveness about the things that really matter.

Are You Ready?

Do you want to explore the lepers' questions? Your situation may be very different from the one the lepers experienced, or it may be eerily similar. You may be . . .

. . . facing a life-or-death health crisis.

. . . financially and professionally successful, but lost and empty inside.

. . . realizing you've devoted your entire life so far to frivolous, meaningless things.

. . . starting a new career, but wondering if it's going to be fulfilling.

. . . hoping to have a better impact on your children.

. . . living to escape instead of living to make a difference in the lives of others.

. . . exhausted, stressed out, and bothered by all the demands of life.

. . . living with gnawing guilt over something you did long ago.

. . . convinced that all the money and stuff you own hasn't brought happiness.

. . . using failures or wounds from the past as an excuse to keep from reaching for the future.

. . . young or old, rich or poor, but aware that there's got to be more to life than you're experiencing now.

Some people are hanging on to hope by a thread. They barely make enough money to pay the bills each month, but a lack of resources is no excuse to live a meaningless life. Mother Teresa and countless others prove that the poorest of people can make a huge impact on those around them—if they notice the needs and care enough to get involved.

Some have gotten a dreaded diagnosis, a call from the hospital or the police station, or have seen their dreams crumble into dust. It appears that all hope has been shattered. It's appropriate to grieve, but it's also time to ask the questions that may have been put off when life was good. Even a few hours, a few days, or a few weeks of renewed purpose are worth pursuing.

Others are at the other end of life's spectrum. By all standards of our culture, they've made it. Yet at some point they wake up and realize possessions, positions, and pleasures can't fill the gaping hole in their souls. They realize they are made for more.

Sometimes people cling to the present because the future is so uncertain. Bobby Bowden was a legendary football coach for Florida State University. As he grew older, writers and fans speculated on his retirement, but years passed and Bowden insisted that he was still up for the demanding job of running an elite sports program. When people openly questioned why he kept coaching for so long, he confided that he had seen what happened to another great coach, Bear Bryant, from the University of Alabama. Less than a month after Bryant retired, he fell dead. Bowden commented, "After you retire there is only one big event left. And I ain't ready for that."

If you are determined to craft a meaningful life, countless distractions and a million excuses are not powerful enough to stop you. If four lepers in a famine-ravaged siege can find a new purpose and make a difference, you can too. For God's sake, don't settle for less. And for God's sake, don't wait. Get up and do something now!

Don't settle for a life devoted to personal comfort and affluence. Open your eyes. See the pain all around you. Let it break your heart, and then invest your time, resources, and passion to care for the distressed and downcast as they become more evident to you.

We are a culture of takers, and we expect everyone around us—family, friends, employers, and government—to make our lives easier and better. When things work out the way we want, we often feel entitled—we think we deserve it. When they don't, we become angry and full of self-pity.

It's time to stop obsessing on our own wants and needs while real people are kidnapped and sold as sex slaves, while millions (including far too many children) die every minute from preventable diseases or lack of clean water, while families are torn apart by addiction, abuse, or abandonment, and while even our close friends live hopeless lives because no one has the guts to intercede and help them take a positive step.

Throughout the world the political left sees government as the answer to the problems of poverty, immigration, climate change, drugs, and the full range of social and economic problems. The political right often appears calloused because they see government intervention as the problem instead of the solution. Those on the right realize that the most effective and efficient forms of charity come from individuals, churches, and organizations that feel compelled to respond. If more people with passion and compassion would step up and help a hurting world, amazing things could happen. It's not about politics; it's about people.

You may not be able to transform world opinion and politics on your own, but as an individual you can do two things: make a difference in your sphere of influence, and support causes that have far deeper and wider impact than you can have on your own. No matter what your situation today, God has a purpose for you—probably a bigger, more sweeping, more meaningful purpose than you have ever imagined.

Please understand that this isn't just a book about leadership, or business management, or character development, or self-improvement. It will touch on all those things, but much more. When a person discovers a sense of purpose, every aspect of his or her life is transformed—every goal, every decision, every relationship, every joy, every disappointment, every obstacle, and every opportunity. Everything.

Let's take a journey with the four lepers as they face threats and opportunities. At each point, they ask crucial questions. Their answers become turning points for them and their whole nation. Those answers, though, didn't come to them all at once. It was a process of discovery, with twists and turns.

It's the same for all of us. We face threats and opportunities, and we're in a continual process of discovery. Sometimes the answers will be clear, but often we will have to dig deep to find them. Trust us: it's worth any amount of effort because it will result in the most rewarding journey of your life.

"For the meaning of life differs from man to man, from day to day and from hour to hour. What matters, therefore, is not the meaning of life in general but rather the specific meaning of a person's life at a given moment."
—**Viktor E. Frankl**

"Everyone—pantheist, atheist, skeptic, polytheist— has to answer these questions: 'Where did I come from? What is life's meaning? How do I define right from wrong and what happens to me when I die?' Those are the fulcrum points of our existence."
—**Ravi Zacharias**

CHAPTER 2

PURPOSE: "WHY AM I STILL ALIVE?"

During the summer and fall of 1940, Germany's air force attempted to bomb England into submission. The city of London was devastated by attacks day and night. Americans who followed the war on the radio were spellbound as they listened to reporter Edward R. Murrow. Night after night, he stood on the rooftops of buildings in central London to describe the situation as bombs fell around him and antiaircraft guns fired into the sky. Today intrepid reporters like Anderson Cooper give firsthand accounts from the world's most dangerous places: Iraq, Afghanistan, Ukraine, and Gaza.

Imagine a CNN newscast with a journalist like Christiane Amanpour explaining what was happening to the four lepers . . .

In the fading light of dusk, the camera pans across the walls of the city and shows the distant tents of the Syrian army. The audience has been following the siege for weeks, maybe months, so the reporter doesn't need to give much background information. She reminds her viewers of the siege and the plight of starving people in the city: "The situation has been desperate for weeks, and it's only getting worse. People are dying by the hundreds in the city. Outside the walls, the poorest people—those who are sick, the outcasts, and the lepers—are facing certain death."

As the camera provides a view outside the walls, it picks up four dirty men in ragged clothes off in the distance, slowing moving toward the enemy camp. What's happening? In search of a story, the reporter and crew sign off, and then hurry to catch up to them. In a few moments the camera comes on again, revealing the four disheveled men who look surprised at the attention, but who are obviously excited. Something has happened . . . something fantastic.

The reporter begins her update: "These men are lepers. They have lived under the shadow of the city walls—ignored and despised. Their situation could not have been bleaker. People inside the city are starving to death, and on the government rationing plan, these men are at the bottom of the list to receive any food. Yet within the span of the last hour, after making a fearless and honest appraisal of their situation, the lives of these four men have changed from utter hopelessness to incredible fulfillment."

The reporter takes one of the men by the arm, and then realizes she has touched a leper. She recoils but stays engaged in the scene and asks the man, "What prompted you to come out here to the Syrian camp? Don't you think that's a little foolish? You're . . . you're just a leper. What hope did you have when you walked into the enemy camp?"

The leper squints as he peers into the lights of the camera: "We had to make a decision. We were thinking: if we stay outside the walls in the leper colony, we'll die, and if we go inside the city, we'll die. Our only hope—and it was between slim and none—was to surrender to the enemy and hope they have mercy on us."

The camera cuts back to the reporter who explains, "The Syrian camp is about a mile from the city. It took these four emaciated, footsore men at least an hour to shuffle that distance. I'm not even sure they have all their toes. They probably stopped several times to rest." One of the lepers on camera nods. "We can only imagine that a strange blend of hope and fear swirled in their minds as they walked." Another leper smiles and nods. "They fully expected to be killed as soon as they arrived, but it was their only option."

A third leper summons the reporter to a nearby tent. The camera sweeps the floor of the tent to reveal piles of gold, platters of food, and fine clothes. The snorting of nearby horses can be heard. The reporter remarks, "Oh my gosh! I'm shocked. Where are the Syrian soldiers? They're all gone! This is totally unexpected." When the reporter turns back to the leper, the man breaks into a huge grin and almost shouts, "We're saved! We're still alive!"

The four lepers weren't sure why they had been spared, but they understood that they were still alive for a reason. Those four men realized an important fact: if you have a pulse, you have a purpose.

A View from the Grave

When people have a fresh realization of their own mortality, they gain a new appreciation for life. Death sharpens our vision of the future.

In 2005, I (Paulus) had a lot of problems with my sinuses. The doctors gave me many different prescriptions for the drainage and headaches, but nothing worked. Finally, they did an X-ray. The diagnosis stunned me: Stage 3 sinus cancer, and the prognosis wasn't positive. I didn't want to die and leave Marliesye, Debbie, Irene, and Timothy. I didn't want to leave the people in our ministry. The only thought reverberating in my mind was, *I will die. I will die. I will die.*

Suddenly, all the things I had taken for granted were in jeopardy. I had made assumptions about the future for my marriage, our children, our extended family, our friends, and our work. In the time it took the doctor to speak a single sentence, all of those assumptions were shattered.

During the following hours, impending death gave me a new perspective on my life. I realized I had taken my most cherished relationships for granted while devoting too much time to my work. I couldn't tell you when my priorities had gone wrong, but now I needed to correct them. When I thought about dying and leaving the people I love, I wept. I wanted them to know how much they meant to me, so I told them—each one, individually and specifically, with the realization that I may have only a short time to let them know.

I had been devoting my best time and energy to my work, but that changed in an instant. I immediately began to give my family my best. I spent time with every member of my family. I told them I loved them, and I apologized for every hurtful thing I had ever said or done. I wanted love to prevail in our relationships—not anger, distrust, or suspicion.

Then I met with our staff to affirm how much I loved and appreciated them. I apologized for taking them for granted and for valuing the organization's success more than them.

In times of trouble, friends are worth more than gold. In fact, when I found out I had cancer, I discovered who my true friends really were. A few people stayed away because they viewed cancer as a judgment from God. Of course, they were wrong. But the ones I'll never forget are the many people who came close. They cried with me and for me. They didn't accuse and they didn't run away. They didn't offer simplistic answers or try to fix my problems. They just loved me and suffered with me, offering me the gift of their broken hearts.

When I was in the hospital, Rich and Melissa Witmer flew from Arizona across the world to sit with me at my Bali bedside. Those two friends took time away from their careers, spent their own money to travel so far, and endured jetlag and strange foods to be with me. I needed them more than I could imagine, and I was humbled to realize that God could send people from halfway around the world to comfort me.

Needless to say, I didn't die from my sinus cancer, and that prompts the question: "Why am I still alive?" I'm still alive for a reason. And God used the threat of death to teach me how to really live.

I had advanced warning of impending death, but sometimes death occurs without a moment's notice. I was on a flight from West Papua to an island in Indonesia. As we waited to take off, a lady named Maria sat down next to me. She was in her mid-forties, a lovely lady who was full of joy. She was on her way to Jakarta, and she was very excited about the meeting she had scheduled. I overheard her call her family and promise to bring back presents.

The plane had been in the air only fifteen minutes when we hit terrible turbulence. As I instinctively grabbed the arms of the seat, I noticed that Maria's face looked frozen. In only seconds the plane found smooth air, so I leaned over to see how Maria was doing. She had stopped breathing, and she was dead. She must have had a panic attack or a heart attack, but she was gone. Suddenly, without warning, Maria passed from the fullness of life to death. I suspect she would have given all the money in the world for just enough time to tell her family how much she loved them. I'm sure they knew already, but she could have expressed her affection with more clarity and passion if she had known this would be her final hour on earth.

As I sat next to Maria's lifeless body, I put my hand on her arm and prayed. The flight attendant asked if I was a pastor. I nodded. She gave me a microphone and asked if I would lead the people on the plane in prayer. I told them that life is short, so we need to make sure we have our priorities straight—with God and with those we love. I prayed for Maria and her family, and I prayed that everyone on the flight would find real meaning in life—before it's too late.

Maria had big plans, and she fully expected to achieve them. She had no idea that day was going to be her last. James, one of the writers of the Bible, warned his readers about making assumptions: "And now I have a word for you who brashly announce, 'Today—at the latest, tomorrow—we're off to such and such a city for the year. We're going to start a business and make a lot of money.' You don't know the first thing about tomorrow. You're nothing but a wisp of fog, catching a brief bit of sun before disappearing."

For some people, life doesn't end quickly enough. Without hope for the future, they simply want to die and get it over with. A man told me that his mother asked him to pray for her death every year on her birthday. He felt terrible about praying such a prayer, but his mother insisted. She made her initial request when she was 83 years old, in bad health, and had difficulty even talking. Every year thereafter on her birthday, she made the same request of her son. Finally, God answered her prayer. She died when she was 106! For those 23 long, empty years, she didn't really live; she only existed. She hoped every day would be her last, and she was deeply disappointed when she woke up each new day.

In contrast, the prospect of death can bring out the best in some people. A couple of years ago, I (Kevin) got a call from my best friend, Garrett. He had just received news that his father had Stage 4 colon cancer and had only months to live. Garrett and I had big, bold plans for our business ventures, but we agreed that he needed to take a step back for a while so he could care for his father. He moved into his dad's condominium in Atlanta, even though his father was fairly independent for the first few months. As the disease progressed, however, his father couldn't take care of himself and needed Garrett to stay close. Garrett had to help him with even the most basic functions, such as going to the bathroom and shaving.

His father's final weeks were, by Garrett's estimation, the most painful and beautiful of his life. He got to say all the things he wanted to say to his father, and in return he heard the things any son longs to hear from his dad. In disease and death, father and son found more meaning than they ever imagined before the diagnosis.

At the funeral, Garrett told the mourners that the last nine months with his father had been a precious gift. Garrett was talking about his father's gift to him, but I'm sure Garrett's presence was a treasured gift to his father as well.

A few people are willing to risk death for a greater cause. Omar was a gifted athlete in high school. He received several scholarship offers from colleges and universities, but he turned them down because he wanted to stay in his hometown with his high school sweetheart, Megan. They got married soon after graduation, and Omar joined the Army. He was deployed three times, twice to Iraq and then to Afghanistan. Between stints overseas, the couple had two children. Near the end of his third deployment, Omar and Megan looked forward to being reunited and enjoying life together. Two weeks before his scheduled return, however, Megan received word that Omar's helicopter had been shot down, and he was killed.

I've always been patriotic, and I admire the sacrifice of all soldiers, but Omar's funeral hit me like a ton of bricks. He had been the best man in my sister's wedding. He was only 26 when he died. He had everything to live for, but he chose a career that daily placed his life at risk. He wanted to live, but he was willing to die. On the day he was buried, I saw the cost of his sacrifice in the faces of his grieving wife and their two small children. It was a heart-wrenching funeral service. An Army officer stood up to talk about Omar, and my brother-in-law Jon shared stories from their friendship. Everyone agreed that Omar was a hero.

I also saw more clearly than ever that living for a purpose bigger than ourselves is more important than life itself. To put it another way, living for a purpose bigger than ourselves is the only thing that makes life worthwhile. Omar's funeral was very sad indeed, but every person there honored a man who had given his life for the cause he believed in. Sadness and comfort are welded together when someone dies with honor. The words of Jesus echoed true that day: "Greater love has no one than this, that someone lay down his life for his friends."

What will people say at *your* funeral? Every day, you craft a life that determines your impact. Every moment, you make decisions that affect the people around you—for good or for harm. It may seem morbid to think about your death, but it's the essence of wisdom to live in light of eternity. King Solomon was perhaps the wisest man who ever lived. He encouraged us to realize that life is a vapor that can vanish in an instant.

The reason we need to talk openly and honestly about death is that it gives us a powerful context to understand the meaning of life. It's not morbid; it's essential. It prompts us to ask the first key question: "Why am I still alive?"

An Empty Life

When we don't live with a realization of death, we may drop off one of two cliffs: some people become frenetically busy, and then frustrated because no amount of activity can fill an empty life . . . and others are bored out of their minds because they can't find enough to fill the hours of each day.

Many people feel completely overwhelmed by what it takes to just get through each day. Single parents have to be both father and mother to their children—preparing meals, helping with homework, driving the kids to school and to practices, and being fully present and effective in their jobs each day. The demands of raising children often conflict with the requirements of being a competent employee with a future in the company. At night they fall into bed and wonder how they can face another day.

It's not just single parents who are frazzled by the incessant demands of life. Many careers measure performance by the number of hours employees devote to the company. Workers look around and see those trying to lead a "normal life" being passed by others who are determined to get the next promotion, so they regularly put in seventy hours a week or more if a project (or the boss) demands it.

For those in business, every promotion compounds the pressures. The additional income, the perks of a bigger office, and a car allowance all feel great . . . but only for a short time. Soon the responsibility of the new role presses down. If they're not careful, it will squeeze the life out of them.

The higher you climb on the corporate ladder, the tighter you hold on because the risk of falling becomes much greater. Money, power, promotions, and awards promise a meaningful life, but they can't deliver. At best, they provide a fleeting kick of adrenaline, but soon reality hits home: life is just as empty with a bigger bank account and a new title as it was when we had our eyes on the next rung up the ladder.

When our hearts are empty, we may try to find meaning in a full schedule. We seem to be in competition to see who can be the busiest. In an article for *Psychology Today*, Jonathan Fields observed the recent shift of response when someone asks, "How are you?"

A few years ago the stock answer was, "Fine," which meant, "I don't want to tell you, so just go away." Today the standard answer is, "I'm really busy," which is code for, "I'm stressed and overwhelmed, but I don't know what to do about it."

Fields describes the lifestyle of a woman named Jan:

> "Jan was becoming more and more stressed and less vested in what she was doing on a day to day basis. And it was taking a toll on her mindset, her health and her life. So, she stepped down to reclaim her own center, her sanity and her health. And along the way, she discovered something she'd always known, but was now in a position to do something about. She was not alone. Tens of millions suffer the life-stifling effects of stress and many of the current treatment modalities are either marginally effective or unrealistic in the context of peoples' lives."

The incidence of suicides and heart attacks is higher on Mondays than any other day, suggesting that people dread facing another week at work. They don't look forward to the challenges of Monday morning. Instead, they become psychologically shaken and physically sick as they face the new week.

On the other end of the spectrum are those who can't find enough things to fill up their lives. They're bored . . . terribly bored. They may have made a lot of money and retired when they were forty, which was their goal in life, but now they can't find enough ways to spend their money to give them anything resembling happiness and contentment. Others don't have much money at all, but they still give up on life, drifting from one day to the next, filling their hours with meaningless television shows and Internet sites. Nothing has captured their hearts, so their only priority is to pass the hours as pleasantly as possible. Some, of course, fill the emptiness with self-defeating mental images and self-destructive actions. They desperately want some excitement, and they're willing to do anything to get it—if only for a few minutes.

Many people have goals, but they're short-term (earning a degree, getting a particular job, getting married and having a family, achieving a promotion, moving to a particular city, etc.). When they reach their goal, they don't know what to do next. They thought reaching the goal would give them ultimate satisfaction, but it doesn't . . . it won't . . . it can't.

Beyond You

People tend to set goals that are too small and too narrow, focused on personal success and acclaim, which never satisfy very long. A true, compelling sense of purpose is always other-centered—it longs to make a difference in other people's lives.

We find a lot of satisfaction and joy in our faith and our closest relationships, but we also need to be certain that *what we do* really matters. We don't have to be astronauts or soldiers, and we don't have to devote our lives to care for orphans or rescue women who have been abducted as sex slaves. Some are called to do those things as a vocation, and many more can play supporting roles in such efforts, but most of us need to realize that what we do each day—even the mundane and ordinary—can be infused with meaning. Every conversation, every meeting, every shovel of dirt, every dish, every nail driven or screw turned, every grand plan, and every small detail gives us an opportunity to do two important things: express our talents, and contribute to the lives of others.

Every person has ability and opportunity. Some are skilled at replacing transmissions, others craft spreadsheets; some are doctors who care for the sick, and others are bankers who loan money so businesses grow and people find new jobs. The possibilities for meaningful work are endless, but it is easy to get sidetracked. We discover true meaning—the reason we are still alive—not when we fulfill *our* dreams, but when we help others fulfill *theirs*.

Now . . . Right Now!

The four lepers couldn't believe it! They fully expected to be dead, but they were still alive! It became their moment of opportunity. They may have wondered if they were dreaming, but they soon realized four people don't share the same dream! What they were experiencing was real. It wasn't an accident of nature, and it wasn't luck that the soldiers were gone and had left the riches behind. All the details of that fantastic moment in history had been orchestrated just for them.

Ask yourself, "Why am I still alive?" Don't wait for the light to dawn on you. Be assertive. Search, explore, discover, and uncover the reason you're still alive today. Author John Ortberg insists that we seize the moment:

> "The greatest moment of your life is now. Not because
> it's pleasant or happy or easy, but because this moment
> is the only moment you've got. Every past moment is

irretrievably gone. It's never coming back. If you live there, you lose your life. And the future is always out there somewhere. You can spend an eternity waiting for tomorrow, or worrying about tomorrow. If you live there, you likewise will lose your life. This moment is God's irreplaceable gift to you."

At first the lepers didn't know why they were still alive, but they assumed there must be a reason. Like them, you may not yet know how to define your purpose. All you need to know at this point is there is a far bigger purpose for your life than you could ever dream. The process of discovery may take a while, or you might already know exactly what it is. Either way, stay with us as we follow the lepers and learn the lessons they teach us.

"Purpose is the place where your deep gladness meets the world's needs."
—Frederick Buechner

"Whatever is at the center of our life will be the source of our security, guidance, wisdom, and power."
—Stephen Covey

CHAPTER 3

MOTIVATION: "WHY DO I DO WHAT I DO?"

Impending death has a way of clarifying one's options. When the four lepers sat outside the city walls, they made an honest appraisal of their situation: "If we don't do something drastic, we're going to die of starvation." It's hard to imagine what it was like for those men to hobble the mile or so to the Syrian camp. Their disease had ravaged their bodies even before the famine. Now the shortage of food had left them emaciated and weak. Every step must have been a challenge. They were motivated, though, by the primal instinct of survival.

When they stumbled into the camp, they didn't see a single soldier. So far so good. They went into the first tent and found a banquet! They ate and drank, and they found a wealth of gold, silver, and clothes. They hid the loot, and then went into a second tent. They quickly gathered all the goods from there, too, and hid them nearby.

After they got enough to eat, their motivation changed from survival to security. If they could amass their own fortune, they calculated, they would never be in such a desperate situation again.

When they returned to the city as wealthy men, they would be the envy of everyone—not just their friends in the leper colony, but of every starving person inside the city. They looked forward to more prestige and popularity than they had ever dreamed possible. The outcasts would become insiders. The despised would become respected. They had it made!

Then one of them suddenly remembered the people suffering in the city. He may have asked himself before he said it out loud: "How can we stay here in the middle of all this wealth and not tell the people back in the city?" When he spoke the words to his friends, they had the same jolt of conscience. Imagine their conversation:

"What we're doing isn't right. We have an opportunity to live for something far beyond our success and comfort."

"This is a day of good news for all the people in the city!"

"Let's go back and tell everyone else what we've found!"

In only moments, the internal compass of those four lepers changed directions. They no longer lived for themselves, but for others who were suffering. Once they realized they weren't going to die of starvation, they took the opportunity to help thousands who were perishing. They wanted to make a difference.

Self-focused motivations may feel completely good, right, and normal at first, but they can never fully satisfy us. Virtually every culture in the modern world values personal peace and affluence, but people have been created in a way that such self-focused pursuits can't fill the gaping hole in our souls. We need a cause that's bigger, more compelling, more challenging, more noble, and outside ourselves.

The Range of Motives

We usually can't identify one single motive that drives what we do each day. Instead, we find a full range of reasons for our choices, some better than others, and some more basic than the rest. Let's look at survival, approval, fun, hidden drives, and calling.

Survival

Abraham Maslow famously articulated a "hierarchy of needs" comprised of five distinct motivations for every person. The most fundamental needs are physiological—food, water, and clothing—and personal safety. These are essential for human survival, but they don't provide meaning, purpose, and hope for the future. Survival instincts are incredibly strong, so they become our top priorities. When basic needs aren't met, people do absolutely anything to find the necessary resources.

Providing the basic needs for ourselves and our families gives us security and dignity. In every culture and in every age, earning a living is a valued motivation. When people can't provide for themselves and those they love, they soon become desperate or depressed . . . or both. When a person has no way to earn a living, he is robbed of dignity.

It was the basic need for survival that drove the lepers to create such a daring plan to approach the Syrian camp. That need was met almost immediately when they found plenty of food to eat.

Meeting our basic needs for survival isn't a bad thing. It's necessary, but it's not enough.

Approval

Maslow and other students of the human condition observe that another important need in every person's life is to feel valued as part of the social system—to be accepted and respected. The four lepers had lost all approval from others, and they certainly suffered for it.

Our place in relationships gives us a sense of identity. While nothing is inherently wrong with the desire to be accepted, we often use the wrong measuring stick. We use comparison to see where we are on the pecking order in our families, in our companies, with our friends, and in our communities. We want acceptance and respect, but we try to achieve those things by being superior to others.

In *Mere Christianity*, C.S. Lewis calls pride "the great sin." Pride, he explains, is fueled by comparison:

> "Pride gets no pleasure out of having something, only out of having more of it than the next man. We say that people are proud of being rich, or clever, or good-looking, but they are not. They are proud of being richer, or cleverer, or better-looking than others. If someone else became equally rich, or clever, or good-looking there would be nothing to be proud about. It is the comparison that makes you proud: the pleasure of being above the rest. Once the element of competition has gone, pride has gone. That is why I say that pride is essentially competitive in a way the other vices are not."

When we meet people, we instinctively size them up as we observe their hairstyle, the brand on their clothes, their shoes, the way they walk, how they talk, and everything else about them. More and better things, we assume, provide a bigger and better identity. But this perspective thrusts people into competition, and we can only feel good if we're winning the comparison game.

In our misunderstanding of meaning, we try to fill our lives with pleasures of all kinds. Paradoxically, some of the unhappiest people are those who have devoted themselves to pleasure. Like an addict who needs more whiskey or cocaine to achieve the same high, these people are driven to buy nicer cars, wear more expensive clothes, and go on more lavish vacations, but the brief sense of excitement soon vanishes into a numbing emptiness.

In another of his books, *Surprised by Joy*, Lewis pondered, "I sometimes wonder whether all pleasures are not substitutes for Joy." He explains that joy is more lasting and isn't based on comparison and pride. It comes from an identity that is secure, beyond the comparison game, and, in the words of Henri Nouwen, "beyond all human praise or blame." We try to make more money so people will admire us. We want promotions so we'll have prestige and power. We wear cool clothes so people will look twice. We live to hear people say particular words when they describe us: *handsome, pretty, successful, intelligent, funny, accomplished, sharp, indispensable*. We want the schools we attend, the cars we drive, the clothes we wear, and the title on our business cards to say we've made it. And nothing is wrong with wealth, popularity, vacations, and awards . . . unless we use those things to climb over others.

Like the lepers, when we realize that the good things in our possession are gifts from God rather than the results of our own accomplishments, we respond with thankfulness rather than competition. And we use whatever we have for a higher purpose—to help others.

Fun

Life isn't supposed to be an endless grind. Certainly, we shoulder responsibilities and face difficulties when we encounter them, but we need a healthy dose of pleasure to make life worthwhile. People do all kinds of things to bring fun into their lives, from gardening to BASE jumping, from riding a bicycle to fishing for marlin, from walking next door to see a friend to flying to the other side of the world for vacation, from watching a movie to writing a screenplay. Sometimes we just want to escape the sameness of everyday life, other times we long to hang out with those we love and who love us, and occasionally, we thirst for adventure.

A quick review of some comments by famous people show the diversity in our pursuit of fun:

> *"Today was good. Today was fun. Tomorrow is another one."*
> **—Dr. Seuss**

> *"It's kind of fun to do the impossible."*
> **—Walt Disney**

> *"Just play. Have fun. Enjoy the game."*
> **—Michael Jordan**

> *"People rarely succeed unless they have fun in what they are doing."*
> **—Dale Carnegie**

"If you go around being afraid, you're never going to enjoy life. You have only one chance, so you've got to have fun."
—**Lindsey Vonn**

"When you have confidence, you can have a lot of fun. And when you have fun, you can do amazing things."
—**Joe Namath**

"I cannot even imagine where I would be today were it not for that handful of friends who have given me a heart full of joy. Let's face it, friends make life a lot more fun."
—**Charles R. Swindoll**

"It's the game of life. Do I win or do I lose? One day they're gonna shut the game down. I gotta have as much fun and go around the board as many times as I can before it's my turn to leave."
—**Tupac Shakur**

"If you obey all the rules you miss all the fun."
—**Katharine Hepburn**

"I realized the more fun I had, the more relaxed I was working, the better I worked."
—**Bill Murray**

"We are driven by five genetic needs: survival, love and belonging, power, freedom, and fun."
—**William Glasser**

Some of the driven, humorless people among us might complain, "Don't be ridiculous. Having fun never accomplishes anything." That's simply not true. Doing things that bring pleasure results in relational, psychological, and physiological benefits. When we do fun things with family, friends, or even strangers, relationships begin or grow stronger. As we participate together, we build bonds of understanding and shared memories.

Pleasure lowers our level of stress, giving us more resilience and usually some distance from our problems so we can think more clearly about them. A little fun, then, is a helpful element when it comes to problem solving. The physical benefits of pleasure are deep and wide. Heart rates go down, blood pressure is regulated, and tension in muscles subsides. Pleasurable experiences stimulate the release of dopamine in the brain, reinforcing the sense of pleasure and increasing the ability to focus so we can repeat the behavior and experience more pleasure. The same thing happens when we perform acts of kindness or generosity. We feel good about it, and we want to do it again. So . . . our brains are hardwired with a feedback loop of fun!

Pleasure is a worthwhile—actually, an essential—component of our matrix of motivation. Don't neglect it! Jimmy Fallon wasn't too far off when he said, "'Have fun' is my message. Be silly. You're allowed to be silly. There's nothing wrong with it."

The risk, of course, is that we'll put too much into our pursuit of pleasure and our lives will get out of balance. Fun is often temporary, and it can be superficial if we're not participating with others. If we take it to an extreme, and especially if we use it to escape the boredom of life, we can become numb, withdrawn, and self-absorbed, missing out on the challenges and relationships that make life meaningful.

Hidden Drives

If we peel back the layers of our motivations, most of us will find some things we hoped would never surface—even though we knew they were there all along. If we're honest, we have to admit that a lot of what we do every day is fueled by hidden drives and shaped by unhealed hurts, unrelieved fears, and unresolved anger. We try really hard to impress people, but inside we feel "less than." We do a lot of really good things, but we may do them for the wrong reasons. It's confusing . . . and discouraging.

At first the lepers had been motivated by survival; they needed to eat to live another day. When they had enough, they looked around and realized the riches they had discovered could give them a measure of significance in the community they had never dreamed they could obtain. They finally realized they were still alive so they could help the starving people in the city. Many people, however, never come to that realization. They remain stuck in a pattern of painful emotions just beneath the surface of their lives. They may be the most popular people in the neighborhood or at work, but they feel like outcasts.

I (Paulus) know how it feels to be an outcast. When I was six years old, my parents divorced. My father had been in the Communist party, so he was already under suspicion in the community. My grandfather was a Muslim imam. After my father left, my mother married a man who already had three children. He didn't want another child, so I was left on my own. I moved from house to house in the neighborhood. I stayed with relatives or neighbors as long as they would have me, and then I moved to another house. In every home, I worked hard to earn my temporary place. For instance, I carried large jugs of water from the river back to the house. In exchange, I received a little rice to eat. Those families took me in, but I knew none of them really wanted me.

When I walked down the street, even as a small boy, I saw the look on people's faces and I heard the whispers, "That's him. That's the boy no one wants." I can identify with the lepers who first only wanted to survive, but secretly longed for acceptance.

When people suffer the deep wounds of rejection, they respond in one of two opposite ways: they either give up on life or they try to earn approval every way they can. I was driven to earn respect. I used every accomplishment to climb another rung up the social ladder. I calculated my words and actions to impress people so they would think well of me. The hole in my heart was a gaping wound, and I tried to heal it by winning the applause of others. Sometimes I got a smile or a nod of respect, which may have been small gestures, but they were addictive. I had to have more. I lived each day to earn a little more admiration from those around me.

The deep hurts of rejection stay with us for a long time. Even as an adult, and after I became a Christian, I have still struggled with my deeply entrenched insecurity and the understandable but misguided motivation to win approval. At some point I realized I was doing a lot of good things—saving orphans, caring for the poor, preaching sermons, and planting churches—for less than noble reasons. To some degree, I was doing all these things to win a smile and earn the approval of those who were watching. I felt driven to work hard and achieve status, which distorted my priorities. I was more devoted to success in my work than to my wife and children. As an unwanted child, I had tried to prove myself every day just to get enough to eat and have a place to sleep. And as an adult, I was still trying to prove myself by being successful. It was very, very hard to see clearly my twisted motivations and be honest about the wounds that drove them, but this painful realization was an important step toward inner healing and real change.

Most of us struggle with motivation to some degree. I have a friend in Australia who was abandoned by his father. The pain he felt drove him to devote his life to proving that he deserved his father's attention and affection. He opened a business and was very successful. He had all the money and power most people could want, but he always wanted more. As he built the business, his income was astronomical and he was featured in business journals, but it was never enough to satisfy him. The drive to be somebody in the eyes of his father consumed him—even after his father had died. Ironically, his thirst to earn his father's love made him a poor father to his own children. His devotion to money and power cost him his own family. When his marriage fell apart and his children wanted nothing to do with him, he came to his senses. He realized the foolishness of his priorities, but he also came to understand the deep hurts that had compelled him so strongly for so long. Finally, he began to change.

Motivations are varied and complex. We may act because we're driven by survival instincts, the desire for approval, the need for fun, or because we experience powerful but hidden drives. These motives aren't wrong or evil, but they're inadequate as the primary, driving force of our lives. There is a higher, deeper, wider, more powerful motivation: a sense of being called to do something that touches the lives of others.

Calling

It must have been tempting for the four lepers to ensure their own futures when they stumbled upon a vast accumulation of unguarded food and treasure. Who would have blamed them for putting themselves first, for a change? Yet in that key moment, they had an epiphany—they had the opportunity to save their entire city by letting everyone else know that the enemy had fled and left everything behind. Now, suddenly . . . shockingly . . . they were in a position they could have never dreamed possible. After long years of being outcasts, they could be heroes. Who could have been more unlikely candidates? Who would have been more willing to risk everything? It was their time. They were right in the junction of desperate need, terrible risk, and fantastic opportunity.

Our life's calling is the cause that keeps us up at night dreaming about what might be, and it gets us up in the morning ready to tackle the challenges. We're willing to make any sacrifice to make it a reality. People often ask me (Kevin) how they can find their calling in life. It's a great question, one that has almost as many answers as there are people. For some, like the lepers, it appears in crystal clarity in a moment, but for most of us, it takes shape much more gradually.

✸ Calling is the intersection of affinity, ability, and opportunity. ✸ If a task doesn't capture our hearts, we certainly won't stay with it very long. If we don't have any aptitude for it, we'll soon quit.

And if we lack the opportunity to invest our time and energies to see something tangible happen, we'll lose interest. But if these three things are part of the recipe, they eventually create a wonderful dish! It begins with a dual realization: "I'm not satisfied with who I am and what I'm doing, and I see something I can do that really matters."

When this happens, a few people will completely change the direction of their lives. They will leave business to go into medicine or law or missions, or they will leave medicine or law or missions to go into business. Not all will change vocations, but everyone will have a new sense that what they do every day has monumental significance. They don't have to be the CEO of a company or a non-profit organization, but they realize their contribution is an essential component in the machine that makes a difference to change lives.

A sense of calling may not necessarily change what you do, but it always infuses what you do with meaning.

For some of us, our calling becomes our career. We work each day in a role that is the center of our calling. For others, our jobs are the platform where we connect with people and build meaningful relationships so that lives are changed. And for many of us, our jobs give us a measure of calling, and our volunteer work completes it. Whether we are paid or not isn't the issue. We are meant to contribute to the lives of others in a way that matters, even at some cost to us. No matter what the price tag, it's worth it.

If our calling is our own idea, we may quit when things get hard, and even if our calling comes from a higher source, there are no guarantees. We will undoubtedly see both marvelous successes and dismal failures. In good times and bad, we give our best. The result of loving service is a wider door to serve more people. As we trust, love, and serve, we are entrusted with more responsibility— we encounter more people with more difficult problems and more complexity in seeing their needs met. The result of good work is more work!

When I see someone like Paulus who is making such a difference, I'm inspired by his example to reach higher and do more because it's so obvious he's right on track with God's calling for his life. If he can find and follow his calling, so can I . . . and so can you.

Calling and identity are two sides of the same coin. Like a compelling sense of purpose, a secure, stable identity comes from outside ourselves. Those who love us speak it into our lives. Those who had loving, affirming parents have a head start on the rest of us, but all of us can hear the voice of God speaking his unconditional love into our hearts. All of us get our identity from something, somewhere, or someone. Even Jesus got his identity from the words spoken by the Father. At his baptism, a voice spoke from heaven, "This is my beloved Son, with whom I am well pleased." The words of identity and affirmation were given before Jesus preached any sermons, healed anyone with a disease, told any parables, or raised anyone from the dead. He didn't start a revolution to gain an identity; he started a revolution from the security and confidence of already having one!

We often get it backwards: we think God accepts us based on our performance, so we try really hard to please him out of guilt or fear that we will lose his love. When we think we're doing well, we're full of pride; when we're failing to measure up, we feel ashamed. But the love, forgiveness, and acceptance of God are his gifts to us. We accept them with empty hands and open hearts, and we're overwhelmed with gratitude that his grace is so wonderful! Then, with a revised motivation, we live to please the one who loves us—not out of guilt, fear, or pride, but in response to his love for us.

God's grace is hard to grasp because we see nothing else like it in the world. School, work, friendships, and clubs function on performance, not unconditional acceptance.

Philip Yancey tells a story about pastor Ian Pitt-Watson, who once commented, "Some things are loved because they are worthy; some things are worthy because they are loved." Pitt-Watson listed the people and things usually admired for their beauty and power: supermodels, athletes, scientists, and works of art. Then he told a story about his daughter's rag doll. Rosemary loved the doll, even though it was worn and dirty. When the family went on vacation, Rosemary insisted on taking the doll along. But as they prepared to board the plane, Rosemary panicked: she couldn't find her doll! Pitt-Watson said the family certainly couldn't leave without Rosemary's doll. They looked for it until they found it, barely making it on the plane before the doors were shut. The pastor later explained that Rosemary's love gave worth to the ragged doll. He noted that God's love for us is like Rosemary's love for her doll: "God's love, thankfully, is not based on our intrinsic worth. It comes by grace, a priceless yet free gift that bestows worth on the most unlovable object. Some things are loved because they are worthy and some are worthy because they are loved . . . we fit in the latter category."

71

Ultimately, we all strive to find a sense of identity. We look in many places, and many of us are still looking. That's not a bad thing. Actually, it's great. Our identity eventually leads to something richer, deeper, and more compelling: finding our true calling—the reason we're still alive and the way we can make a difference in the world.

It's wonderful to see people live out their calling. My friend Billy Richardson was in the airline business for many years, but he left to become a teacher. He makes far less money, but he is totally fulfilled as he pours himself into young lives. He told me he gets up every day with the gut-level confidence that being an educator is what he was meant to do with his life.

A young lady named Elizabeth turned down a job paying twice what she's making in her role managing details for a leadership development organization.

Richard was on track to go to medical school, but his heart was captured by the plight of orphans around the world, so he's now the managing director of an adoption agency.

Sarah is the CEO of a small IT company. She has created a work environment that values integrity, communication, and mutual affirmation as much as profits. Her employees, from the top executives to the custodian, love being part of the company. She always reminds them that what they do makes businesses run more efficiently so fathers and mothers have better jobs to provide for their families.

Calling has nothing to do with a person's level of income. I've seen a parking attendant treat people with courtesy instead of grumbling at his seemingly boring job. He realized every interaction is an opportunity for him to touch a life, no matter how briefly or lightly.

On the other end of the socioeconomic spectrum, Horst Shulze is the former president of the Ritz Carlton hotel chain. Their in-house slogan is, "Ladies and gentlemen serving ladies and gentlemen." He now runs The Cappela Group, an equally impressive company with hotels around the world. When a hotel opens, he goes for a week to train the entire staff, from the top managers to the dishwashers in the restaurants. He focuses more on the "why" than the "what" of their jobs. He asks them, "What do you want people to say about us when they leave after staying at this hotel?" In the hotel industry, they want to be known as the best. Mr. Shulze doesn't try to produce excellence in his staff by intimidation or monetary rewards, but by appealing to a higher sense of calling: to create an environment that honors every person on the property. He always says, "We don't hire people. We select people." To him, there's a big difference. Hiring is simply filling slots on the organizational chart to get tasks completed. Selection focuses on the character of the person, the fit for the organization, and the compatibility with the hotel's values. Mr. Shulze is looking for men and women who are called to the same excellence of service that runs through his veins.

Added Value

Some of us may feel called to use our talents in a realm we never before imagined. Billy Payne played college football and went to law school after his playing days were over. He became a successful attorney in Atlanta, Georgia. He enjoyed his role, but he felt there was something more. Billy wasn't looking for a new idea or some grand vision, but his church asked him to lead the fundraising campaign for a new building. He had never done anything of the sort, but he agreed to try and the campaign was very successful. On the Sunday the new building was dedicated, he felt a deep sense of accomplishment. He enjoyed seeing his church community come together, and he wondered what it would look like to do something similar for an entire city.

After seeing success at his church, Billy's dreams got a lot bigger. He finally decided to try something truly audacious: bring the Olympic games to Atlanta. He had never organized anything that big in his life, but he felt called to give it a try. He began meeting with people, crafting plans, and organizing a bid for the Summer Olympic games. A few years later, the Olympic committee met in Tokyo and announced that Atlanta would be the site of the 1996 Olympic Games. Billy Payne's experience as a teammate in college and his role as an attorney prepared him for something more.

After the games were successfully held in the city, Billy reflected, "So many people have assumed I had this great motivation as a civic-minded leader, that the growth of the community and jobs and the tax base was important to me. Those things never crossed my mind. Now, having said that, a lot of big stuff has happened since the Olympics, but as a consequence, not an objective. What stands out for me is the legacy of possibility."

A person's calling may be as large as bringing a city together for a greater purpose, or it may be to bring a family or a team together to accomplish something bigger than themselves. Calling is always challenging. It inspires dreams. And it's always focused on making others' lives better and comes at a cost to those who are called.

But the reward of seeing lives changed more than compensates for the price we pay. We know our efforts have made a difference, and we sense God's smile.

All religions—Muslim, Hindu, Buddhist, Jewish, Christian, and all the rest—encourage their followers to live beyond themselves and pursue transcendent purposes. When we can look back on our lives and know we've made a difference, we have a deep sense of satisfaction. In the upside down view of life, the secret of personal happiness is to give, sacrifice, and care for others.

If you're still alive, you have a purpose. A purpose may begin with broad outlines, but sooner or later it takes the specific shape of a calling. A calling usually exposes conflicting motivations: some noble and right, others colored by fear and pride. We have the opportunity to choose our motives and invest our lives in things that matter. And with that, we have a sense of satisfaction deep in our souls.

When they got to the first tent, the lepers thought finding enough food would satisfy them, but it didn't. It only gave them strength to hide the treasure. Then they thought the treasure would give them the status they longed for, but it wasn't enough either. They suddenly realized they had a higher purpose, a deeper calling, a wider reason to live. Now they were ready to take action.

"I arise in the morning torn between a desire to improve the world and a desire to enjoy the world. This makes it hard to plan the day."
—*E.B. White*

"Calling is a 'yes' to God that carries a 'no' to the chaos of modern demands. Calling is the key to tracing the story line of our lives and unriddling the meaning of our existence in a chaotic world."
—Os Guinness

CHAPTER 4

RESOURCES: "WHY DO I HAVE WHAT I HAVE?"

It was a stunning reversal of fortune. The four lepers walked away from the city as pitiful victims of a prolonged famine. The human body initially responds fairly well to hunger, with weight loss as the first symptom, but soon, to produce energy it begins to consume muscle and other vital tissues. The body quickly breaks down and suffers a cascade of problems. Vitamin deficiency often leads to a variety of diseases, which can then produce the multiplied effects of fungal infections, diarrhea, and heart failure. The lack of water initially causes intense thirst, but this normal, healthy sensation eventually subsides. Without the driving desire to drink water, the person suffers dehydration, as well as physical and mental exhaustion. For healthy people who face the onset of a famine, the consequences are devastating. But these four men already had the dreaded disease of leprosy! They were more susceptible than most to the ravages of famine.

When they pointed their bandaged feet toward the enemy camp, they had nothing but the dimmest hope that someone might have mercy and give them a scrap to eat. Yet when they entered the first tent, it was like Christmas, a birthday party, and a national holiday all rolled into one! They ate and drank their fill. They might still die, but it wasn't going to happen on this day! Then they looked around at all the things the soldiers had left behind. They grabbed all they could hold and ran out into the desert to hide it.

In Indonesia there's a saying, "Aji mumpung," which means, "This is our opportunity. Get as much as you can—right now!" That's how these men felt as they cleared out the first tent and then the second one. Suddenly ... and unexpectedly ... for the first time in a long time they had more than they needed. But it was still not more than they wanted.

After probably a half an hour of grabbing as much as they could hold and hiding it for the future, one of them had an amazing insight: Maybe finding all this stuff wasn't just for the four of them. Maybe, just maybe, it was for thousands of others in the city who were slowly dying of starvation and disease. Those people, you'll remember, had kicked the lepers out of their city because they didn't want to be around their dread disease. The lepers had a chance to care for people who hadn't cared at all for them. The things in their hands (and hidden in the bushes) could change their world. But they immediately realized the tangible things weren't the most important. It was an intangible—the news about the empty camp—that would make a much bigger difference.

Natural Inclination

No matter how much we have, human nature drives us to long for more. We're seldom satisfied, so we try to stack up, store up, and save up as much as possible. We assume that having more—more money, more possessions, more time, more toys—will give us the comfort, protection, and prestige we long to acquire.

A certified financial planner regularly asks new clients an insightful question: "What does money mean to you?" He said that the vast majority of people give one of two answers (and when he talks to couples, the two spouses often give different answers). Having plenty of money gives most people either *security* or *pleasure*. A bulging portfolio of investments is attractive to one group because it assures them they won't be in need. Maybe they were poor when they were children, or they may have suffered bankruptcy earlier in their careers. Whatever the cause, that group values financial security above all else. The other answer reflects a very different perspective. Fear doesn't drive those people; comfort and excitement are their purposes in life. They want enough money to have the finest possessions, extravagant travel destinations, and a pampered lifestyle.

The natural inclination is to view possessions (including all resources: money, things, time, and connections) through self-absorbed eyes focused on security or pleasure, even though we know that financial freedom doesn't always bring fulfillment. In fact, a person can be fabulously wealthy but desperately poor in heart, or a person may have very little of the world's goods but have a full and thankful heart. The rich person feels impoverished and craves more, but the poor person who is filled with love and purpose feels like a king or queen!

When we find ourselves with a wealth of possessions, positions, and passions, we naturally want to use them to make our lives easier, better, and more fun. But there is a higher purpose for the gifts we have been given, other than hoarding them all for ourselves.

Many people have closed fists. They're afraid that if they give, they'll lose those things forever. They haven't discovered that generosity is one of the greatest joys of life. If we give with joy, we always get back far more than we gave—not necessarily the same type of things we gave away, but always much more. We may give money and receive the delight of knowing we've given an orphan a better life and an education. Or we may give time to listen to an elderly person, and we get the satisfaction of knowing those minutes made her feel special. Whatever we choose to give, greater meaning always comes back to us—and it's well worth it.

There's nothing inherently wrong with wealth. Jesus didn't condemn rich people for being rich, but for being selfish with their possessions. David Nicholas is a financial planner who is committed to help his clients make as much money as possible so they can use it to advance God's purposes. Many clients come to him without a clear perspective of using their wealth for purposes bigger than themselves, but David teaches them, inspires them, and gives them direction to connect their money (and time and talents) to causes that change lives for eternity.

The lepers realized they suddenly possessed a resource far more valuable than the gold they found in the tents. It was information. They knew something that could change the lives of starving individuals, families, a city, and a nation. They could keep the information to themselves, or they could choose to give it away.

A Process of Change

Most of us need some time and experience to realize our possessions can be used for a greater purpose. For fifteen years Kyle Williams was dedicated to building his business in Enid, Oklahoma. As he reflected on those years, he told me (Paulus) that all his efforts during that time were to prove himself by increasing his power and income. Success made Kyle feel invincible, and he thought he could take whatever he wanted, but his drive for success came at great cost. He was unfaithful to God and his family, and consequently, his wife, Carol, left him. In the next three years, his business suffered.

God sometimes uses our mistakes and failures to get our attention. During the time when Kyle was broken and alone, he became a Christian. Almost immediately, he called Carol and asked to meet with her. He apologized for his selfishness, and he asked her out for a date. Carol was suspicious, but she agreed to go out at least once with him. Kyle gradually regained her trust, and after a while the fires of their love were rekindled, and they got married again.

Kyle also started over again in business. With God's blessing, his interests expanded. He soon owned over twenty-seven gas stations and convenience stores, radio stations, restaurants, emergency care clinics, and interests in the oil business. I met him several years ago, and we became good friends. He invited our family to come to his home for a vacation. One night at dinner, my skeptical daughter Debbie asked him "Mr. Williams, I'm curious. Why do you care so much about my father and his work, and why did you pay to have our family fly from Indonesia to Oklahoma? I understand that you are very rich, and you are very generous. What is that about?"

Kyle smiled, "I want to know your dad and your family better. I finally understand that God gave me wealth, not to increase my *standard of living*, but to increase my *standard of giving*." wow!

Kyle gives generously to many different causes in his city and around the world. He believes his wealth is not really his own, but something that passes through his hands to allow him to make a difference in the lives of people in need.

Casual observers might assume the Kyle Williams who built his successful business before his divorce and business reversals looks a lot like the Kyle Williams who enjoys business success today, but the two are polar opposites. In his early years, no amount of wealth gave him satisfaction and peace. However, after God changed his heart, he was content even in the lean years before his new ventures began earning an income. And now that he's generating wealth again, he hasn't let it corrupt his heart. Kyle now has an open hand both to receive blessings and to distribute those gifts to countless others. Kyle Williams is thrilled to play a small role in changing one life at a time.

When we give time, money, talents, or anything else, we may struggle with both inner doubts (*Is it really worth it?*) and outspoken critics who think we're crazy for being generous. In the business world, competitors may think we're weak if we donate any resources instead of leveraging every dollar to earn more profit. Our friends and neighbors may think we've lost our minds for spending time visiting prisoners, feeding the homeless, or caring for the elderly in a nursing home. "What can they give you in return?" they wonder silently, or maybe even ask to your face.

The measure of our giving isn't what people can give back to us—that's a negotiation, not a gift. The true value of giving is that we give expecting nothing in return. Only then will the returns be far bigger, and often far different, than anything we anticipated.

Greed doesn't die a natural death. It has to be acknowledged and have the life choked out of it—aggressively and continually—or it will come back to haunt us. No one has to teach a child to be selfish; it's the standard operating system for human beings. And our cultures—American, Asian, European, Australian, and all the rest—reinforce the desire to have more and better things. Advertising has a powerful impact on us. The purpose of advertising is to create discontent and then offer a promise that a product or service will fulfill their desires.

In his book, *The Technological Society*, Jacques Ellul observed,

> "One of the great designs of advertising is to create needs; but this is possible only if these needs correspond to an ideal of life that man accepts. The way of life offered by advertising is all the more compelling in that it corresponds to certain easy and simple tendencies of man and refers to a world in which there are no spiritual values to form and inform life. When men feel and respond to the needs advertising creates, they are adhering to its ideal of life. The human tendencies upon which advertising like this is based may be strikingly simpleminded, but they nonetheless represent pretty much the level of our modern

life. Advertising offers us the ideal we have always wanted [and the ideal is certainly not a heroic way of life]."

Ellul's observations should make us stop and pay attention to all the messages we see and hear each day. The "ideal" life depicted in modern advertising promises to fulfill our extravagant expectations of plenty, popularity, and pleasure. In contrast, the "heroic" life is one of honor, duty, sacrifice, and joyful service to others. Why is our image so important? Dale Carnegie stated succinctly, "You are not dealing with creatures of logic, but creatures of emotion, creatures bristling with prejudice and motivated by pride and vanity." Greed crowds out heroism.

Greed makes us fools. People sacrifice the most valuable things in life—their relationships with God, their spouses, their families, their friends, and sometimes their health—to have more things that can't possibly bring true fulfillment. The thirst for more promises plenty but inevitably leaves us empty.

Sensitive, reflective people may overreact to greed by going too far in the other direction. They feel guilty for having things, so they get rid of money and possessions as soon as possible. They may appear generous, but that type of giving is driven by guilt and fear, not love and joy.

I (Kevin) know people who feel very uncomfortable with the things they possess. In fact, some of them avoid taking jobs that pay well because they think it's somehow beneath them to make a good living. They struggle over buying even the basic necessities and live in a self-imposed prison cell of guilt. I believe people like this are mirror images of the blatantly greedy—both groups are poor stewards of the talents and resources God has entrusted to them. If they weren't shackled by fear and guilt, they would have the joy of receiving good things from God and gladly passing much of it along to others in need. They're missing wonderful opportunities to make a difference, and they're impoverishing their own souls in the process.

Sarah's family wasn't particularly wealthy, but they weren't poor either. For some reason, she grew up feeling very uncomfortable with having money in her pocket. She's a very sensitive person, and she believed it wasn't right for her to have money, and the things money could buy, when others were poor. Her mother had an incredibly hard time getting her to go shopping. Finally, her mom stopped trying. Instead she brought new clothes home so Sarah could pick what she was willing to wear, and she always chose the cheapest, plainest ones.

Sarah went to college, got a job, and married Will, but her emotional allergy to money didn't change. In fact, now she had more money to prompt her guilt. She still wore drab, cheap clothes that she often bought at Goodwill. Will tried everything he knew to get her to "loosen up." Gradually, very gradually, Sarah began to realize that having money wasn't a sin, and having a few nice things wasn't a character flaw. She began to understand that everything could be received as a gift—and enjoyed instead of prompting intense feelings of guilt and shame. She learned that receiving is the prerequisite to giving.

Sarah's brother Jonathan had the opposite problem. He never saw a dollar that shouldn't be spent. Jonathan's closets, drawers, and every corner of his room were full of stuff: clothes, games, toys, and sports equipment. When he got older, he earned more money to acquire even more stuff. (Sarah and Jonathan probably fed each other's behavior, but we'll leave that for a family therapist.)

Internal change requires honesty. Guilty people have to realize their lives have been dominated by fear and that it's not wrong to have things. Their possessions give them opportunities to love, give, and serve they would never have if they were poor. And stingy people have to recognize the emptiness of hoarding the things they possess—many or few. When they clinch their hands to hold things tightly, they squeeze the life out of those things, and they can't receive anything else.

There are no happy guilty people and there are no happy stingy people because fear dominates happiness. Guilty people can't sleep when they think they have too much, and stingy people can't sleep when they think their neighbors have more than them. Both groups are sad to see happy people, and they are happy to see sad people. There has to be a better way, and God has given us one.

Full Hearts, Open Hands

No matter whether we grew up in the poorhouse or a mansion, we can learn to make the right assumptions about our possessions. When I (Paulus) was a child, I had nothing, absolutely nothing. My normal human reaction was to try to acquire as much as possible and hoard all I could find. After I became a Christian, I still struggled with my faulty assessment of possessions. Gradually, I learned to see things from God's point of view. Now, when I drive by a huge mansion, I'm not jealous. I think, *Twenty years ago, Marliesye and I didn't have a home, but now we have one. I'm so thankful for it!*

When people eat, they use only one fork, not two and not ten, no matter how many forks they own. When they get dressed, they wear only one set of clothes, whether they have a dozen closets full or only one outfit. Why does anyone have more than he or she needs? It's simple: to share with those who are without.

Some people have little to share because they're too proud to receive good gifts. Their hearts remain in poverty because they've closed them off to the love and generosity of those around them. Nasarudin Hoja is a wise man from Persia. One day he went to the local outdoor market and discovered the place was in chaos. Everyone had crowded onto the riverbank. Somewhere up the river, a man had fallen into the water, but the current was so strong that he couldn't get to the bank. Nasarudin watched as dozens of people leaned over the river and shouted, "Give me your hand!" But the man didn't reach out. He kept tumbling in the water toward his death.

Nasarudin realized the problem wasn't that the drowning man *couldn't* reach out, but that he *wouldn't* reach out for help. He ran down the bank ahead of the man, leaned out and commanded, "Take my hand!" The man immediately reached out and grabbed Nasarudin's hand and was saved. He had been too proud to receive help from countless people on the bank, but finally became fearful enough to take my friend's hand.

Many people are like the drowning man. They pride themselves on not needing anyone or anything, and they aren't good at receiving gifts. When they refuse to receive, however, they have nothing to give away. The unwillingness to receive always results in poverty of spirit . . . and sometimes pride leads to death.

Gratitude opens the floodgates of generosity. The perception of our circumstances changes from "never enough" to "more than enough." We give, not to impress anyone, and even when no one notices. But we can be sure there is always One who notices. When we give generously with no strings attached, we feel a deep sense of satisfaction.

Some might say, "I have so little that it won't make any difference whether I give or not." One day in the temple Jesus saw an old widow give two cents. Her gift may not have impressed the rich people walking past her, but it made Jesus sit up and notice. He pointed her out to his disciples and told them that she had the heart of God. Even if we have no money at all, we can give our time, our attention, our listening ears, and our smiles. Those are wonderful gifts to the people we meet each day.

A few people insist, "I can't give now, but I'll give when I'm rich." It seldom happens that way. Riches rarely transform self-absorbed people into generous ones. Acquiring more money and possessions only makes them more protective of what they have. Learn the joy of giving when you have little, and if you ever become rich, you'll be generous with great wealth. Start now. Give what you can, and see the results.

Others worry, "What if I give to people who misuse my gift?" We need to give with equal doses of wisdom and compassion. A reporter conducted a study of people standing on street corners holding signs asking for donations. He found that many of them were actually drug addicts, and that every dollar given to them was used to buy drugs and continue a destructive habit. But those people are in need, aren't they? Yes. However, if we really want to help them we can donate to agencies that help people overcome their addictions and live responsible lifestyles. Wise giving may take a little more research, but it's far more effective.

Generosity is *addictive* . . . in a good way. When we give, we sense God's pleasure, and we see our gifts make a difference in people's lives. We donate our time to read to children, and we see the joy in their faces. We give our sweat to build an orphanage or clean up a sick person's apartment, and we realize we've made someone's life a little more comfortable and safe. We contribute money to a church or some other organization, and we watch as men and women, boys and girls, are drawn into a relationship with God, experience his grace and strength, and find new purpose for their lives. And we can't wait to give again!

Generosity is also *contagious*. When we see the joy others get from investing their hearts, time, talents, and money in life-changing ventures—and especially if we see a group of them doing it together—we want in!

Greed multiplies a sense of entitlement ("I deserve more") as well as comparison, competition, and resentment. Generosity multiplies love, joy, and gratitude. It's your decision. Choose wisely.

Do Something!

Take some time to imagine how God might use you and the things he has put in your hands to make a huge difference. You can partner with an existing organization, or you can start your own. The sky's the limit! Ask God for a big vision, and see where he takes you.

But don't dawdle while waiting for all the details of your dream to come together. Use what's in your hands today. Wash the dishes (without being asked). Visit a lonely person. Bake a pie and take it to a discouraged friend. Call your parents (without complaining to them or asking for anything). Smile at the gas station attendant, the person sitting near you at work, or the clerk at the store.

Not long ago, I (Paulus) was at the airport for a very early flight from Bali to Jakarta. I went into the restroom before boarding the plane. The man cleaning the restroom looked bored and discouraged. I smiled at him and gave him $2. Then I shook his hand and told him, "Thank you for your work. This is for your breakfast."

Instantly a big smile swept across his face. He looked at the money and then back at me and said, "Thank you! Thank you! Thank you!" My gift was very small, but it made a big difference in that man's morning. His joy was his gift to me.

When I got on the plane, I sat next to an attorney. He asked me what I do for a living, and I told him I'm a pastor. We talked about our respective roles. Before we landed, he handed me an envelope. I had no idea what was in it. After we walked off the plane and said "Goodbye," I found a quiet spot and opened the envelope. It had $200 in it. I was like the man in the restroom earlier that morning: I had received an unexpected gift—a gift from God that had passed through the hands of a man I just happened to meet.

Money, as we have seen, isn't the only currency of giving. We can express love and care in many different ways. Pastor Agus, the director of Mercy Home orphanage in Soe-West Timor, got a call one day that a five-year-old girl had just become an orphan. Elda's father had never been around, and her mother left soon after her little brother was born. Her grandmother tried to care for the two children, but she was too old to work. Starvation led the grandmother to a fateful decision: to kill the two children and herself. Elda walked into the room where her grandmother had been taking care of her brother. She had suffocated him between her legs, and she had died, too.

Elda lived alone for several weeks before Pastor Agus got the call that she needed help. He went to the village to bring Elda back to the orphanage. Three weeks later, I asked how the little girl was doing. Pastor Agus said, "Elda is very sad. She hasn't smiled since she's been here."

I flew to the island and went to the orphanage. The director brought Elda to me, and I held her for a long time. Finally, I looked at her and saw a big smile. She finally felt safe and loved. Elda's new joy filled my heart. For weeks, I was buoyed by the memory of that little girl's smile. Later I brought her to Bali, to our orphanage, where I now see her every day. When our eyes meet, I have a joy that money can't buy. I gave love to her, and she has given great delight to me.

The radical generosity of people touches us almost as deeply as God's unlimited kindness. Years ago, Garrett, Robbie, Courtney, and I (Kevin) had a dream to launch an organization to take college students around the world to change their lives. Our first trip was planned for Africa, especially so Garrett could visit an orphanage to see Martin, a boy he met years before who inspired him to start a charity. We had a big dream, but we had no money to pull it off. We hosted a fundraiser that was the most polished, professional, passionate event I've ever seen—yet the people who attended didn't give much money. We were far short of our goal. Garrett was sure the money would come in from somewhere, but a week before we left for Africa, we were still a long way from our goal. Garrett met with Jesse Peel, a mentor and friend, to ask for advice. Jesse gave more than that. He wrote a check for the entire amount we needed for the trip, and he called it a loan. He said, "You can pay it back tomorrow, in a year, in five years, or never. I just want to help."

We were, to say the least, ecstatic, and the trip was a huge success. A few years later, I got to know Paulus, and I had another dream. I wanted people all over the world to hear his message and be exposed to his heart. I wanted to write a book with him, but I didn't have the money for the expenses of traveling to Bali to meet with Paulus and hiring an editor to help me with the manuscript. Garrett called me one day and asked if we could go to lunch. He said he had some things he wanted to talk about.

When we sat down, Garrett reminded me of the generosity of Jesse Peel, and he handed me a letter he had written:

> I remember a time in my life when I would have given anything to head back to Africa to see Martin and bring a team of best friends to form a new company along with me. I remember sitting across from an old man, Jesse Peel, who looked me in the eyes and told me he believed in our dream. He pulled out his checkbook and wrote a check for an unimaginable amount of money to make the dream possible—a loan that seemed preposterous and built on nothing but faith. I told myself that at some point in my life, I wanted to do the same thing for someone else who had only a wow idea and faith that it would make a difference. I think you and Pastor Paulus are the ones for that.

Garrett wrote a check to cover all the travel and editorial expenses for this book. He was paying forward the generosity Jesse Peel had shown a few years before.

So dream big, take a step, and let generosity multiply in you and through you. If you make a lot of small decisions to give your time, money, possessions, and effort, it will be easier to keep doing so when the stakes are much higher—as in marriage, raising children, and all the other important sacrifices in life.

The true value of a gift isn't defined by the giver, but by the receiver. The two dollars Paulus gave to the man in the restroom wasn't much to Paulus, but obviously meant a lot to that man. Jesse Peel's loan to Garrett and the rest of us was somewhat significant to him, but it was life changing to us. You have this book in your hands today due to the generosity of Jesse Peel and Garrett Gravesen.

At least one of the lepers realized he had more than enough, and he wanted to use the surplus God had given him to help people in the city who were dying from the famine. His friends recognized the opportunity, and together, they saved the city.

Like the lepers, we can do something—something important—now!

"We make a living by what we get, but we make a life by what we give."
—**Winston Churchill**

"You can give without loving. But you cannot love without giving."
—**Amy Carmichael**

CHAPTER 5

FRIENDS: "WHO IS GOING WITH ME?"

Friendships make life meaningful. In fact, none of us can reach our potential without the honesty and support of good friends.

When we look at the story of the four lepers, we see a remarkable relationship. Who knows how many years they had lived outside the protection of the city walls? In the ancient Middle East, their disease wasn't viewed as simply a physical problem; people believed it was the result of a moral failure. They were kicked outside the city because the people didn't want to be contaminated by their sins (they assumed) or the stench (which was very real). As outcasts, condemned and despised, the four men needed each other so they didn't spiral into depression and death.

It would be very interesting to speculate how a documentary film team on the site would portray the events of this story. The director would show the effects of the famine in the city, the horrible condition of the emaciated lepers, and the powerful Syrian army only a short walk away. We wouldn't have to wonder how bad the conditions were for the lepers outside the gates. If the film crew caught the conversation among the four friends, they would have seen and heard an interesting interchange. The four men had no rosy illusions. They were brutally honest with each other. Blind optimism may not hurt anyone in good times, but it's deadly in a crisis. They objectively analyzed their situation: "If we stay here, we'll starve to death and die. If we go into the city, it's no better there. We'll starve and die. Our only shot at survival is to do the unthinkable: go to the enemy camp and plead for mercy."

The writer doesn't tell us if these four men lived among a group of ten or fifty or many more who faced the same predicament. In fact, a large group may have been part of the initial discussion, but in the end, only four made the decision to leave the gates of the city.

The four men were filled with equal parts of fear and courage. After they reluctantly decided to proceed, the camera would show the men nod in agreement, sigh deeply, stagger to stand up, and take the their first steps out onto the rocky terrain. Every step hurt. Toes had either already fallen off or broke off on this hike. Malnutrition and dehydration made the chronically sick men even weaker. When one had to stop, they all stopped. If one thought about quitting, one of the others gently took him by the hand and helped him stand so they could take a few more steps. If one had doubts and said, "We're fools for doing something so stupid!" the others didn't argue. They simply reminded him, "It's our only hope."

They were struggling for their lives, but they were struggling together.

After a while, the men were exhausted. The sun was going down, but in the last light of day they saw the tops of the Syrian tents. Until this moment, their plan had been all theory and concepts, but now reality was setting in. Very soon they would know if they would live or die.

We can imagine one of them pointing to the tents in the waning light. The others looked, and then without a word, they nodded to each other. And they took another step. Now fear and courage intensified.

The documentary surely would capture the puzzled look on their faces when they stumbled out of the bushes into a camp that was deserted but full of food and riches. It was too good to be true! They gorged on delicious food—better than anything they had eaten since they were first forced to leave their families because of their disease. They laughed and marveled at each bite. Their next inclination was to store up as much as they could put their hands on. Nothing would ever be the same!

Their friendship took another turn a few minutes later. One of them said, "Man, look at all this. We're rich!"

Another one had a different expression on his face. "Yeah, but think about where we came from. Those people back in the city..."

A third stood up from where he'd been hiding stuff in the bushes. "We don't really need all this. And besides, where would we put it? We don't live in houses. We live beside a wall!"

The last leper looked at the second one and announced. "You're right. We should leave it here and go back to the city to tell them what we've found."

"I don't know," the first guy slowly shook his head. "This is the first time in my life I've had more than I needed."

"Then you stay here," the fourth leper told him. "Or take your part and leave ... or do whatever you want. We're going back."

"Oh, all right. I'll go with you," the reluctant one finally told the rest. "Maybe my stash will still be here later."

Together they had departed with scant hope; together they would return with the news of a miraculous rescue. They were friends at every turn in the story.

West and East

In Western cultures, and America in particular, people want to see themselves as brave, self-reliant men and women who don't need anyone or anything. This conception may have come from pioneers who left the safety of their homes and families to venture into the unknown, yet they almost always went in wagon trains with many others.

In the business world we look back at the titans of the past—Andrew Carnegie in steel, John D. Rockefeller in oil, J.P. Morgan in banking, and Cornelius Vanderbilt in railroads—or we marvel at people in modern times who have built corporate empires—Steve Jobs, Warren Buffett, and Bill Gates. We mistakenly assume that these people (and others like them) have made it entirely on their own. Yes, they are brilliant, and yes, some of them are often ruthless, but most of them have stood on the shoulders of others who shaped their lives, imparted values, and supported them during lean years.

The inherent misconception of rugged individualism is that it's possible to be unaffected by the people around us. We may want to believe the support and wisdom of others don't matter, but they do. They always do. In an interview about his book, *Outliers*, Malcolm Gladwell explained,

"We have fallen in love with this notion of the self-made man, of the rags-to-riches story, of the idea that if you make it to the top of your profession . . . you're the one responsible for getting to the top. . . . And that idea and that ethos has permeated virtually every way in which we think about achievement, and I think that that idea is completely false; it's worse than false, it's dangerous!"

Various cultures around the world have very different values and perceptions of the importance of relationships. People don't make major decisions without the input and support of their families and friends. The process of give-and-take almost always takes longer than a single man or woman making an individual choice, but the community supports (instead of criticizes) the final decision. For instance, a couple doesn't just decide to get married. They have a long courtship so the extended family and friends can meet and interview the prospective partner. This may seem odd and laborious to people from the West, but Indonesian rates of divorce have traditionally been lower.

In every aspect of life—family, business, friendships, and service—we are far more effective if we have supportive, encouraging partners. The process of making decisions takes longer, but people seldom feel alone when they encounter difficulties later on. In the West, people expect to make choices by themselves, so they often feel inordinate pride when things go well . . . and ashamed and isolated when they fail. In Indonesia the community offers the collective wisdom of age and experience, and people readily accept input from others. After the plans are implemented, they are not

BIBLICAL

left alone. People "rejoice with those who rejoice and weep with those who weep."

Broadly speaking, Indonesians see the people close to them as pillars of support, but in the West we often see them as competition, or perhaps as stepping-stones to be used to advance our lives and careers. If we see people this way, we're always on guard, and people around us often feel used instead of valued.

The four lepers demonstrate a healthy and right perspective of relationships. They formed a cohesive community, supporting each other, prodding each other, and sharing with each other. When they realized they had enough, they didn't compete to accumulate even more. They trusted the unconventional wisdom of the one who suggested they should share with the people in their city—the same people who had ostracized them and kept them outside the city gates because they were lepers. To those four men, caring for the broader community was more important than personal gain.

Three Kinds of Connections

We function most effectively—and happily—when we have three spheres of meaningful relationships: peers who walk beside us, mentors who have walked before us, and those we help to walk their own paths.

Peers include friends, spouse, and business partners. They are usually about the same age and at a similar place in life, so they intuitively understand when we talk about our dreams and struggles. They may be able to "finish our sentences" because they know what we're thinking, and they don't laugh or run away when we're honest about our doubts and difficulties.

Mentors may be teachers, professors, parents or grandparents, coaches, counselors, or supervisors in business. We may have a natural connection with them, or we may hire them as executive coaches to help us take the next step in our careers.

At a pivotal point in the development of the business Garrett and I (Kevin) had built, Todd Williams stepped in to give us the benefit of his wisdom and experience. Todd is twenty years older than Garrett and me, but he understands exactly what we're trying to do. We initially asked him to give us some advice about our structure and direction, but after a few months it became obvious that he could offer us much more than occasional input. We asked him to be the president of our company, and he graciously accepted. He has insights into people and processes that Garrett and I would have gained in a couple of decades, but we need his wisdom now! Todd is a great gift to us and to the people we influence. He makes us much more effective than we would be on our own.

You may have a lot of acquaintances, but you probably have only a few friends you trust with your deepest secrets. And you may have only one mentor who helps you blossom as an individual and leader, but the right one is plenty good enough.

In my work, I have a lot of opportunities to pour myself into other people. We have a talented staff team that is passionate about helping businesses and brands create initiatives that enhance leadership and social impact. It would be easy to just use our team's abilities to grow our own business, but I want to do more than that. I want to invest in our team members and their futures—the way a few mentors have invested in me. I want to give them a platform to learn, grow, and excel. I want to help them clarify and begin to fulfill their own dreams, not just the goals of our organization.

In the American business world, many people in positions of middle management don't believe they're ready to help anyone—perhaps as the youngest person at their level of the company, or maybe itching to take the next step of promotion. Either way, their eyes are still riveted on their careers, not those beneath them on the organizational chart who could use their help to grow and learn. You're never too young to help others, and you don't have to be on the list of "The Top 100 Most Influential People" to make an impact. You can probably name people right now who desperately need someone to care and help them navigate the often-murky waters of corporate life.

To make connections, initiate some conversations with the people in your office, especially those who are just starting out. Ask them about their hopes and dreams, and then listen. Really listen. Don't rush to give advice, but keep asking great questions to draw them out. Sooner or later, they will realize you care about them as people instead of just pieces of the organizational machine, and they will want you to give them input on every aspect of life.

When we can answer the first three questions—Why am I still alive? Why do I do what I do? And why do I have what I have?—we view the people around us through a different lens. We no longer see them as competitors, but as human beings with hopes and hurts, people who long to find meaning and want their lives to count, people who are inherently asking the same questions we have asked. Like us, they desperately need answers, and we are now poised to help them.

We have a purpose, a calling, and resources to invest—and people around us would love to learn from us. First, though, they need to be convinced that we care about them. Giving too much advice too quickly makes them feel like projects instead of people. Listen a lot, and offer advice sparingly. If they know you care, they will be sponges that soak up all you have to offer.

I (Paulus) have mentors for my marriage and my ministry. Mike Murphy and his wife Valery have helped Marliesye and me when we have struggled in our relationship. They can help because they've been there before us. Mike and Valery had difficulties early in their marriage, and someone helped them. They passed their wisdom and love to us, and now Marliesye and I can pass along those insights and hope to those who come to us for help.

The quality of one's life is directly dependent on the quality of relationships in all three spheres: friends, mentors, and those who are helped along the way. We need to choose wisely because our choice of friends and mentors will determine our destiny, and we need to shrewdly select the right people into whom we invest our time and advice.

Marliesye and some pastors are my peers who know me well. Marliesye and I walk shoulder to shoulder in our marriage and in our ministry. At any time and for any reason, I can call the pastors who have become close friends.

Rich Witmer is the man who came to visit me in the hospital when I had cancer years ago. We've been very close for many years. I really enjoy the letters, emails, and phone calls with him. Occasionally we get to see each other face to face, even though he lives in Arizona. It is such a delight to be with him. We talk, laugh, and cry together. His wife Melissa is a close friend to Marliesye. Richard Green is another dear friend. Richard is a bright man, a real thinker. He challenges me to think more deeply, and I enjoy our interactions. I have several other dear friends in Australia and Indonesia who are treasures to me.

Our organization includes orphanages, radio stations, and a leadership school that are overseen by more than ninety staff members. A few years ago my perspective on those people changed. I realized they aren't in my life just to make our ministry more successful. I now believe they are in my life so I can help them achieve their destinies, to help them take the next step from where they are to where God wants to take them. Their goals have become my goals, and I love to see them stretch and grow. Some of them couldn't speak English a few years ago, and now they are translators when Americans or Australians visit us. Some had lived hopeless lives in refugee camps, but now they have purposeful, important roles in our organization.

I've learned to avoid being possessive of our staff members. They are God's people, not mine. Some come to us for a season, and others for a lifetime. I never know how long people will stay with us, so I need to be willing to let them go wherever they are called.

When staff members turn forty years old, I sit down with them and ask, "Are you happy in your role? Do you feel like you are serving at your maximum capacity and effectiveness? Is this role your true calling?" I explain, "By this point in your life, you really need to be in your true calling. If this isn't it, I'll help you find it." These conversations often confirm what people are already doing, but sometimes the employees realize they no longer fit their current role and responsibilities.

Not long ago I had this conversation with a very gifted and faithful man, and he realized God had called him to be a pastor instead of directing one of our orphanages. I told him, "Our ministry is a transit site for you. Most people don't stay with us until they die. Like you, most people come for a while, and when they find their true calling, they go. I'll help you in every way I can. If I can provide a place for you to grow while you're here, I'm happy to do that. If I can then provide resources for you to go somewhere else, and if I can help you serve at your maximum capacity, it is my joy." I gladly released him and helped him find the right place to serve as a pastor. I am thrilled to see men and women identify their God-given calling and serve in it with all their strength, creativity, and joy.

Sometimes Marliesye and I marvel at the growth of our staff members. When they feel led to go to another ministry, it's hard to see them leave. We've invested so much in them, and it's our natural inclination to want to keep them with us. But we look at each other and remind ourselves, "They are the Lord's, not ours." We release them, bless them, pray for their success, and search for the next person to train and love. That's our role.

In *Good to Great*, a classic book on business leadership, Jim Collins explains that relationships trump everything. Choosing wisely is "putting the right people on the bus." Then we can experience "a great life" of fulfillment and achievement. Collins wrote,

"For no matter what we achieve, if we don't spend the vast majority of our time with people we love and respect, we cannot possibly have a great life. But if we spend the vast majority of our time with people we love and respect—people we really enjoy being on the bus with and who will never disappoint us—then we will almost certainly have a great life, no matter where the bus goes. The people we interviewed from the good-to-great companies clearly loved what they did, largely because they loved who they did it with."

I'm always aware that people are watching me—how I treat my family, how I treat our staff, how I treat the students at the orphanage, how I respond to difficulties, and how I maximize opportunities. I don't live in a cave; I live in a fishbowl. This reality is both the highest privilege and the heaviest responsibility of my life. People intuitively sense pride and fear in those who lead them. I hope they will sense something else in me: trust in the goodness and greatness of the God who has called me to follow him.

The Power of Friendship

Meaning, fulfillment, and joy in life always come through people. From a secular perspective, meaning is maximized through relationships. When I look at the ministry God has given us, I'm amazed to see the scope of it all: 12 orphanages, 44 radio stations, over 1500 churches planted, and a new television program. All of this began through a remarkable relationship and has grown in the fertile soil of friendships. My family and I were stuck in a refugee camp. We were just a few more statistics in the war between Muslims and Christians, forgotten in the backwater of battle.

But Rod Plummer cared enough to come to see us, and he provided the money to move us from the camp to Bali, first to a hotel and then to a rented house. I don't know what would have happened to us if Rod hadn't been such a friend.

Rod had been a mentor to Mike Murphy. When Rod told Mike about us, Mike invited us to go to Australia to speak at his church. At the time, we had no church, no building, and no ministry . . . only the hope that God might open some doors for us. I spoke to a small group at Mike's church and told them about our dreams. While I spoke, a man got up and left the room. After I spoke, he found me and said, "Pastor Paulus, God wants me to help you with your ministry. While you were speaking, I felt God leading me to write you a check. Here it is." He handed me a folded check. It was for $10,000! It was enough to begin our ministry in Bali.

That moment didn't happen in a vacuum, and it didn't occur by magic. People's hearts were touched and they wanted to partner with us. They were—and they are—true friends. And it didn't stop there. Those friends have continued to talk to their other friends about us, and those new friends support us so we can do even more to reach people and care for orphans, the poor, and the forgotten. All these friendships have a purpose. They make us feel good and give us comfort, but they also help us take steps to fulfill the biggest dreams we can ever imagine. Everything we do, everything we are, and everything we will become is because we have been given such wonderful friends.

True friends know when to comfort us and when to prod us. They care enough to ask the hard questions, confront us when we give evasive answers, and tell us the truth about our past, present, and future. Amazingly, God has given me (Kevin) this kind of friendship with Paulus. In the time we've spent together, we have become very comfortable, but it's not a superficial comfort. It's the kind of relationship that is so secure that I can let my guard down. Paulus asks penetrating questions—not because he's trying to confuse me, but because they are the same questions he asks himself. His questions make me wrestle to find good answers.

For instance, he asked where I want my business to go in the next five to ten years. If some people asked this question, I would be hesitant to answer because I might wonder about their agenda. Do they want to use me and my organization as a rung to climb higher in their careers? But I know Paulus doesn't have any agenda like that. He is truly probing to help me clarify my goals and plans, and I deeply appreciate his involvement in the process.

Paulus has a gentle, almost offhanded way of prodding me. He always invites me to dream bigger dreams, to think deeper thoughts, and stretch for more than I had imagined. When a new, challenging goal surfaces, I can come up with a dozen excuses why it can't work, but Paulus just smiles and asks, "Why not?"

Take a Look

In some ways we're constantly evaluating our friendships to see if we're on track with them, but it's easy to make too many assumptions about the people we hang around. It's a good idea to regularly evaluate the condition of those relationships. We might see a broad range, from inspiring . . . to comforting . . . to neutral . . . to phony . . . to toxic. Who are the people who challenge you to be your best, and who are those who drag you down? On the other side of the equation, who are those on whom you are having the most positive influence, and in whose life are you little more than dead weight? (Yes, it might hurt to be honest, but it's necessary.)

Someone may not be a bad person, but he or she may be a bad influence on you if somehow the chemistry isn't right. Realism is a virtue, but pessimism is a drag. When the two of you are together, perhaps you become more negative, critical, and pessimistic . . . or you do foolish things you wouldn't have done on your own.

Are your friends calling you to your highest and best, or do they bring out your lowest and least? What kind of person are you when you hang up the phone or walk out the door? Are you better or bitter? A true friend may say hard things to you, but he will encourage you to respond with courage instead of giving up in fear and self-doubt.

Every person who steps into our lives is there for a purpose. The noble and good ones challenge us to be our best; the negative and critical ones test us and force us to respond with more wisdom than ever before. Both can have a positive impact on us, but only if we have insight and courage. However, we don't have to embrace them equally. If we make toxic people our best friends, it's foolish to expect to thrive as we pursue our goals. Every person can teach us something, but not everyone will be our friends and partners. We must choose wisely—especially in marriage—but in *every* relationship.

The people who travel with us will have a dramatic impact on our journey and will determine whether we arrive at our destination. Even people who may support you can make the journey a pain. You know the kind of people who are difficult to ride with for six hours in the car: you all arrive at the destination, but you wish you could have slept for most of the trip.

If the four lepers had picked the wrong people to join them on the journey, they may not have arrived at the enemy camp, and they may not have turned back to save the city. If even one of them had been negative and hopeless, he may have poisoned the minds of the other three. These four had a remarkable friendship, one that changed the future—first for each other, and then for an entire city. If they hadn't supported and encouraged each other, we would never know their story, and history would have been altered. Their choice of friends made all the difference for them, and it does for us, too.

Don't be too quick to jettison the people who don't make you feel great about yourself. They may be in your life for a different reason: so you can help them. Loving them will come at a price. You'll have to overlook some things that annoy you, and you'll have to endure hard conversations that are unpleasant. The person may accuse you of being too harsh when you speak the truth or not caring when you need some space. But your courageous love may eventually change the person's life. If we avoid people who are annoying or difficult, we miss out on some wonderful opportunities—for their change and our growth.

The most important—and often the most difficult—decisions in our lives are about relationships. It is right to invest time to love a difficult person, at least for a season or until the person rejects our efforts. But we can't afford to weigh our lives down with demanding, judgmental people and expect to reach our goals. Be loving, but be wise. Invest in a lot of people, at least for a while, but be very selective about your closest friends.

Every person has inherent value, but you may not be the right one to help a particular individual reach his or her goal in life. You can't take everyone with you to your destination. You can help a lot of people take some steps on their journeys, but only a very few will walk a great distance with you on yours.

In times of difficulty and heartache, we find out who are friends really are. When the ministry in Indonesia was growing very fast, some leaders who felt threatened by our growth confronted me (Paulus). In their jealousy over the organization's success, some people accused us of unspeakable things. At a crucial moment, a friend of mine stood up and took a big risk to defend me, but he believed in our mission and me. He confronted my accuser and said, "I've known Paulus for many years. I trust him. You can believe him."

After that experience, I thanked my friend for defending me, and I went to my accuser and thanked him for playing an important role in my spiritual growth. If I hadn't faced that test, my faith wouldn't have gotten stronger. Through the test of his opposition, I grew. (I think he was more than a little surprised when I thanked him.)

A country song by Tracy Lawrence describes the kind of friendships that matter. The chorus goes like this:

You find out who your friends are
Somebody's gonna drop everything
Run out and crank up their car
Hit the gas, get there fast
Never stop to think "What's in it for me?" or "It's way too far"

They just show on up with their big old heart
You find out who your friends are

Investing time and effort in relationships provides tremendous returns. The return on investment may not be in dollars, but certainly pays off in personal growth and development. We know our investment is profitable when we see people make better decisions, respond in faith to life's difficulties, and chart a bold path for the future. And they know their investment is paying off when they see progress in our lives. Investments always involve risk, and smart investors know when to go "all in" and when to be cautious.

The lepers left the city empty handed, but they soon had more resources than they could use. They realized they had options.

We, too, have more options than we normally imagine. We have many kinds of resources, but they're not only for ourselves. We can become wise investors in the lives of those around us. And also, we need to make sure we have the right people investing in our lives.

"If you go out looking for friends, you're going to find they are very scarce. If you go out to be a friend, you'll find them everywhere."
—Zig Ziglar

"People with deep and lasting friendships may be introverts, extroverts, young, old, dull, intelligent, homely, good-looking; but the one characteristic they always have in common is openness."
—Alan Loy McGinnis

CHAPTER 6

BAGGAGE: "WHAT AM I CARRYING ON THE JOURNEY?"

Standing in the deserted Syrian camp, the four lepers faced a choice. They had come out of sheer desperation after living in poverty, disease, and impending death for a long time. Their chances of survival had been between slim (if they dared approach the other camp to beg for mercy . . . and a little bread) and none (if they stayed outside the city gates or tried to go inside to join the rest of the starving people). To their utter amazement, the soldiers had fled, leaving all kinds of food, clothing, and riches. The four men first devoured as much food as they could eat, and then grabbed armloads of stuff to hide. They were rich! For the first time in their lives, they had enough. No, more than enough. They had plenty.

Yet as soon as one of them pointed out that it was wrong for them to keep their secret to themselves when other desperately hungry people needed this food, the others agreed to go back to the city. Perhaps they looked at their stash of goods and asked themselves, "Hmmm. I wonder how much of this we can carry.

We barely made it here on our diseased feet and legs, and we weren't carrying anything! If we try to carry all this back, we won't make it."

They faced the choice of keeping everything they had found to spend on their own comfort and prestige . . . or leaving it behind for a bigger purpose.

The historian who chronicled this event describes only one thing the lepers carried back to the city, the one essential thing— the good news that the Syrians had fled, leaving everything else behind!

The men shuffled back down the road toward the city. When they got to the gates, they called out to the sentries with the startling news: "We went to the enemy camp last night, and you won't believe what happened. The entire camp was empty! The soldiers were gone, and they left everything . . . everything!"

The sentries may not have believed that four ragged, starving, stinking men could have walked so far, and they must have been incredulous when they heard the news, but they sent word to the king to give him the message. The king first feared the Syrians had implemented a plot to trick them to come out of the city, so he sent scouts on two of the few remaining horses.

A few hours later, the scouts returned with magnificent news. The lepers' reports were true! The enemy had fled all the way to the Jordan River, discarding even more clothes and equipment as they went! When the people heard the news, they ran, hobbled, and crawled to the enemy camp. The siege was lifted, the famine was over, and the people were saved!

Repack Zone

The first time I (Paulus) flew to Singapore, I was surprised to see a crowd of people standing at long tables in a corner of the airport beneath a sign that read "Repack Zone." They had come to the airport ready to fly to their destinations, but while checking their luggage had discovered a bag over the weight limit. In some cases, the extra cost of an overweight bag is more expensive than the plane ticket. One lady told me the airline was going to charge $1000 for her bag!

The people had to make the decision to pay the extra expense or remove some items to lighten the load. Many people in the Repack Zone looked very unhappy. They had to leave behind articles of clothing, hair dryers, gifts, books, food, and other things they had carefully packed for their journey. Their trip wasn't starting the way they had planned.

The first time I (Kevin) took college students overseas for a study abroad program, the weight limit the airline set for a single checked bag was fifty pounds. We had informed all our students about the airline's policy, but one young lady must not have read the memo (or maybe she assumed no one would notice). At the check-in counter in Atlanta, she could barely hoist her bag onto the scales. It weighed 110 pounds! In this case, the airline didn't offer the option of paying an additional fee for excess weight. If she didn't get her bag down to the weight limit, she simply couldn't go with us.

Her parents had come to the airport to see her off. The three of them opened her bag and went to work. For the next thirty minutes tears streamed down her face as she took out shoes, clothes, and other things she had been so sure she needed for our trip. Over and over again, she zipped up her bag and put it on the scales. Each time it was still too heavy, and she had to take more things out . . . prompting more anxiety and more tears. Finally, she achieved her fifty-pound limit. The moment was marked with equal parts relief and sorrow. I'm sure she thought she would run out of clothes after a few days, but she made it just fine.

First, Identify Your Destination

The lepers' questions are sequential. They begin with purpose and motivation, and then move on to include an analysis of resources and the selection of companions. The final of the five questions concerns our "luggage": what are we carrying on the journey?

If we don't know our destination, we won't know what to carry. It would be absurd to take snowshoes and a down-filled parka on a beach vacation. If we're going on business trip, the clothes we pack will be very different than the ones we would take on a surfing excursion to Bali. The destination dictates the choice of baggage, and sometimes people have to make major adjustments so they can get to where they're headed.

A young couple set a goal of saving enough money to make a down payment on a house. When they reviewed their spending and saving habits, they realized they were spending far too much money on entertainment and eating at fine restaurants. If they continued at their current pace of spending on those things, they would never make it to their goal.

A young woman got a degree in nursing, and she began a promising career. After a few years, however, she had a sense that nursing wasn't the career of her dreams. She applied for medical school, and was accepted. After more years of med school, internship, and residency, she is now a practicing pediatrician. When her destination changed, she had to make a whole host of decisions about her time, her income, and her expenses. The sacrifices, she was convinced, would be worth it.

A businessman established his career as a mid-level executive in a nationally respected company. He made enough money for his wife and three children to live comfortably, and he volunteered at his church. After a presentation by Compassion International about helping poor people in the far corners of the globe, he and his wife began supporting the ministry. They gave more and more to the organization because the living conditions of the children tugged at their hearts. After several years, the man began hinting to his wife that he would like to work for Compassion International. He contacted the organization to find out more about the opportunities, and a month later he and his wife flew out for an interview. During those months, their hearts were moved, so their destination changed.

This man had been on a promising career track toward a comfortable retirement, but everything changed when God put kids on his heart. Suddenly, many of the things he and his family had taken for granted were no longer as important. In fact, some of the things they thought were essential became hindrances to their new direction. They had to jettison habits, priorities, and possessions so they could do what God now called them to do. With a new vision and passion to care for tens of thousands of needy children around the world, those things suddenly seemed very unimportant.

Our destination usually includes three components: family, career, and the other things that give life meaning (friends, service, hobbies, etc.). Our calling doesn't always make all of these components line up perfectly. Quite often, we pay a price to do the one thing God has put on our hearts. We may need to sacrifice income, time, prestige, or comfort—and a few committed people even sacrifice their lives. To reach our destination, we will have to make choices, often very hard choices. Invariably, we realize at least some of the things we've been carrying must be left behind. We believed they were valuable, but they have become excess baggage for our journey.

If we ask the question about baggage before we identify the destination, the question seems intrusive, offensive, and ridiculous. We have no context for sorting all the things we carry. We have no grid for making the necessary decisions to throw away some things and keep others. The questions about purpose and destination must come first, but when the destination becomes clear, we naturally look at everything in our hands to see if those things will help us get where we want to go.

⚹ Many people are waiting for someone else before taking action. They want others to make them happy, fulfilled, and comfortable, and ultimately to define their destination for them. The few people who manage to live charmed lives of plenty without lifting a finger or ever making hard decisions usually live shallow lives without any driving purpose. The vast majority of us have to do our own hard work of clarifying our purpose, defining our destination, and sorting through our baggage. It's difficult, but it's necessary if we're going to grow wiser and stronger so we can make a difference.

Too often, people expect their spouse, employer, parents, or friends to make life meaningful for them, but life doesn't work that way. We have to find our own happiness, so much that it overflows to the point where we have enough to share. However, most of us aren't happy because we still carry unrelieved hurts from the past.

Replacements

Hurt people hurt people. If we haven't resolved the wounds we've acquired from past relationships, we will bring those pains (and demands and defensiveness) into every relationship for the rest of our lives. When we're under stress—which happens often in families and at work—we naturally resort to coping styles that were formed from our deepest wounds. Some of us *fight* back, some *flee* and run away, and some *freeze up* emotionally. We may reflect on a disproportionate reaction to an event and wonder, *Why in the world do I respond like this?* But it doesn't take a psychologist to figure it out. We only need to peel back the layers of our life's history to reveal unhealed wounds that continue to cause pain, sometimes decades after the events occurred.

If our hurts aren't addressed, they inevitably produced unhealthy baggage of resentment, self-pity, grudges, superiority, and worry. Whenever the wounded person thinks of the offender, he clinches his teeth and hopes the person will have to pay for what he's done. But anger often has a companion: self-pity. Wounded people have been victims of abuse or abandonment, but the unhealed hurt changes their self-concept. Sometimes they see themselves as permanent, intractable victims of injustice. They feel completely justified in their anger, which festers into long-held grudges. They feel superior, insisting, "I would never treat anyone like she treated me!" In their insecurity, they live with a foreboding sense of anxiety, wondering when they'll be victims again. People who continually carry such burdens discover they are far over the weight limit for a happy, fulfilled life!

Many of us need a "repack zone" where we can identify and remove any such excess baggage that's weighing us down, costing too much, and preventing us from getting where God wants us to go. The problem is that by believing we're victims, we remain passive and don't make any progress. It's someone else's fault! And holding grudges feels so right.

Bethany grew up in an alcoholic home. Until she moved away to start a new job in a different city, she lived in the strange world that fluctuated between chaos and silence—outbursts of anger from her drunk mother and explosions of rage from her exasperated dad, soon followed by an eerie quiet when everybody acted like nothing was wrong. Bethany internalized the craziness, and keeping all that hurt, fear, and anger inside made her alternately numb and driven. She thought leaving home would solve the problem and give her relief. It didn't. Wherever she went, her pent-up emotions would bubble up and create problems.

A few years into her new career and new life, the backlog of painful emotions overwhelmed her. She was dating a nice young man, but she couldn't connect with him. Something within her kept pushing him away. She became confused, then frantic, and then depressed. A friend finally broke through the hard crust of her heart and exposed some of the pain she had been carrying. Bethany realized she had been living with—and feeling completely justified about—enormous amounts of self-pity over how badly she had been treated, and she was filled with bitterness toward her parents. With the help of her friend, she began to repack the contents of her heart. It was the hardest thing she'd ever done, and the most important.

Over time, the ever-present pain within those who have been hurt over and over again will consume them. They often become bitter . . . at those have hurt them (and that list continues to grow) and at God for not protecting them from the hurts. Bitterness gives them identity and energy. They think of themselves as "the one who was wronged," and the desire to see those who hurt them suffer in return gives them a reason to get up every morning. They don't see their perspective as wrong or sinful. No, they justify their attitude because they fully believe that person deserves to be punished.

Author and philosopher Lewis Smedes observed that many people don't understand forgiveness. They assume something magic happens and the pain just goes away—along with the memory of the painful events. But forgiveness always involves the process of grieving and healing that leads to renewed hope. He explained,

"Forgiving does not erase the bitter past. A healed memory is not a deleted memory. Instead, forgiving what we cannot forget creates a new way to remember. We change the memory of our past into a hope for our future."

Letting bitterness, self-pity, grudges, and anxiety remain in our hearts isn't just foolish; it's destructive. Some experts suggest up to half of all hospital admissions are the result of physical symptoms related to stress. Carrying emotional baggage contributes directly to high blood pressure, heart disease, and many other stress-related illnesses. And this baggage has an indirect but negative effect on many other diseases.

Quite often, people fight the wrong battles. In Indonesia, poisonous snakes occasionally bite people. News reports sometimes describe how the person who was bitten spent several minutes trying to find and kill the snake instead of seeking immediate medical attention for the poison. During those minutes, the poison often does its deadly work, and the person dies. People who willingly carry emotional baggage are like those snakebite victims. They spend their time and energy trying to kill the reputations of the people who have hurt them when they should be much more attentive to the poison of hurt, fear, and anger coursing through their hearts. They may not die physically, but they die emotionally, spiritually, and relationally—becoming hardened and numb, unable to give or receive love.

Whenever we detect the destructive baggage of unrelieved hurt in our lives, it's time to do some repacking. We need to forgive the person(s) who hurt us, grieve the loss we experienced, learn the lessons God wants to teach us, and thank him for the love, wisdom, and joy that will return as the hurt is healed. The old saying, "Forgive and forget," is impossible in one sense. We don't get a lobotomy when we forgive people who have wronged us. We will still remember the events, although the sting can be removed from our memories so that we no longer think of that person as "a liar," "a cheater," or "the one who betrayed me." We begin to love flawed people, and we realize that's how God loves us.

If we insist on carrying excess baggage of unrealistic expectations, demands, anxiety, and resentment, we may not make much progress toward our destination—and in fact, we'll probably have the wrong destination. We will want relief instead of meaning, self-protection instead of significance, and revenge instead of purpose. When we get rid of that baggage, we travel lighter, we have more fun, and we make a lot more friends along the way. Like the student at the Atlanta airport, we may shed some tears as we unpack all the things we've been carrying, but we then have the opportunity to go somewhere exciting and meaningful.

Real People, Real Choices

Sometimes the wounds we feel are self-inflicted. We perceive ourselves as "less than," inferior, and unworthy of attention. When I (Kevin) arrived as an undergraduate at the University of Georgia, I met many friends who were third or fourth generation UGA students. Many of my peers came from a long academic legacy, but I would be the first person in my family to graduate from college. Some of my classmates had big trust funds to fall back on; I had only the trust of my parents that I could succeed.

To minimize the amount of student loans I needed, I worked at a retail store in the mall near my home. To be honest, I was embarrassed that I had to work while I was in school. I remember driving home on weekends to get in some hours. During Christmas break I had to work even more. I always hoped none of my classmates would walk into the store and see me working there.

For a while, I carried the baggage of perceived inferiority. I lived with a nagging, constant anxiety that someone might find out that I was an outsider. I didn't want to say anything that screamed, "I don't belong here!" But neither did I want to shade the truth to appear more acceptable.

In my case the excess baggage wasn't a personal wound from the past; it was an insecure identity. For a long time, I attempted to compensate by trying harder and pretending I had the same resources as others. Finally, I decided to get rid of the problem: not the *reality* of my history, but my *misguided perception* of that reality. At some point I realized my history was a source of strength, not weakness. I didn't need to compensate for any deficiency. Instead, I could celebrate the fact that I was charting a new path for my family. It was my honor to be the first to make it through college. With this new insight came a new self-concept—not because my history had changed, but because my analysis had changed. And from there I developed a life-changing perspective: A fulfilling future comes from a renewed view of the past.

Nelson Mandela had every reason to be bitter. He had been imprisoned on Robben Island off the coast of South Africa for over a decade before the authorities allowed him to see his wife and daughter. At the time, he had no idea that he had served less than half of the 27 years he would be in prison. When apartheid was finally overturned, many politicians across the world expected a bloodbath of reprisals. Mandela refused to let the bitterness of the past color the prospects of his nation's future. When he became president, he implemented policies that fostered reconciliation, not revenge.

The movie *Invictus* depicts Mandela's role in smoothing the tension between the majority blacks in the country and the predominately white national rugby team, the Springboks. Only a year into his presidency, Mandela attended a game between the Springboks and England. He realized many of the blacks in his country were cheering for England instead of their country's team. Many politicians insisted the team change its colors and name to be more sensitive to the blacks. Mandela disagreed. He didn't want the rugby team and its white fans to be treated with the same contempt he had experienced under apartheid. When the team won the 1995 Rugby World Cup, Mandela proudly wore the team's colors and celebrated the victory—a solitary black face among tens of thousands of whites.

At Mandela's funeral, U2 lead singer Bono celebrated his legacy:

> "It was he who rebooted the idea of Africa from a continent in chaos to a much more romantic view, one in keeping with the majesty of the landscape and the nobility of even its poorer inhabitants. He was also a hardheaded realist, as his economic policy demonstrated. To him, principles and pragmatism were not foes; they went hand in hand. He was an idealist without naiveté, a compromiser without being compromised."

And former British Prime Minister Tony Blair recalled his impact:

> "Mandela made racism everywhere not just immoral but stupid; something not only to be disagreed with, but to

be despised. In its place he put the inalienable right of all humankind to be free and to be equal."

Mandela's long, grueling, senseless imprisonment could have ruined him, but he allowed it to make him. When he got out, he chose to forgive and to seek unity with the people who had wronged him. His experiences—and the wisdom and love hammered out on the rocks of Robben Island—prepared him to be one of the most influential leaders of the 20th century.

Extending forgiveness and reconciliation is never easy after being egregiously offended. Many times it isn't powerful opponents from outside that create our biggest problems, but our own family members. Such was the case with Joseph—a biblical figure who, like Mandela, ended up in jail undeservedly.

Joseph was Jacob's (Israel's) eleventh son. He was his father's favorite, and his brothers hated him for it. Jacob gave Joseph a beautiful coat, one that was so distinctive that it only alienated him further from his jealous brothers. One day when Jacob sent Joseph to check on the other boys who were tending the sheep, they were angry enough to kill him. They threw him into a well as they hatched their plot, but when the opportunity presented itself, they decided instead to sell him to a passing caravan and get a few dollars for their brother. Then, to cover their merciless act, they killed a goat, smeared Joseph's coat with its blood, and told their father a wild animal had killed him. Jacob was grief-stricken, but the brothers were sure they'd seen the last of Joseph.

The caravan took Joseph to Egypt where he was sold to one of the pharaoh's royal officials named Potiphar. Joseph was an excellent servant and a handsome young man. Potiphar trusted him to run the entire household, but as time passed Potiphar's wife repeatedly tried to seduce him. Each time Joseph refused. The spurned woman eventually accused him of attempted rape, and Joseph was thrown into prison.

The warden soon realized Joseph had remarkable administrative talents, so he put him in charge of the prison. For about fifteen years, Joseph ran the place. At one point, the pharaoh's cupbearer and baker were thrown into jail. Both of them had dreams while there, but had no idea what their dreams meant. Joseph volunteered to interpret them and correctly predicted that the cupbearer would soon be released and restored to his position, while the baker would be executed. Joseph asked the cupbearer to remember him to the pharaoh, but he soon forgot all about Joseph.

A full two years later, the pharaoh himself had two troubling dreams, and his magicians couldn't make sense of them. Only then did the cupbearer think of Joseph. He told the pharaoh about the prisoner he used to know, and a messenger was sent to summon Joseph to the palace.

Joseph accurately analyzed Pharaoh's two dreams: seven years of abundant crop growth would be followed by seven years of famine. Joseph recommended that Pharaoh place a competent person in charge of storing grain during the good years to prepare for the famine to come, and the pharaoh could think of no better person than Joseph. In a moment, the former prisoner became second in power in all of Egypt and in charge of the country's economy. When famine struck, the Egyptians had enough to eat, but other areas were not prepared—including Canaan, where Joseph's father and brothers lived. They were starving to death, so several of the brothers traveled to Egypt to buy food.

When they arrived, they didn't recognize the man in charge as Joseph, and he didn't tell them who he was at first. He first wanted to determine if they had changed for the better over the years, and he created a series of tests to see how they would respond. When satisfied, he finally revealed himself to them, and they were astonished. The pharaoh invited Jacob and his family to move to Egypt, and the family was saved.

Joseph hadn't taken anything tangible with him when he was sold to the caravan; all he had was his integrity. And he hadn't taken anything with him when he was thrown into prison; all he had was his tenacious faith. He refused to wallow in self-pity and bitterness all that time (about thirteen year total), and when a big opportunity arrived, he was ready. He had trusted that somehow God would make things right in the end.

After their father Jacob died, Joseph's brothers were afraid Joseph would execute them. He reassured them, "Don't be afraid. Do I act for God? Don't you see, you planned evil against me but God used those same plans for my good, as you see all around you right now—life for many people. Easy now, you have nothing to fear; I'll take care of you and your children."

An attitude like Joseph's will prevent our wounds—even the worst ones we might endure—from infecting the rest of our lives. Joseph didn't let bitterness become baggage that prevented him from reaching his destination.

We can't find a way to insulate ourselves from all pains in life. If we try too hard to isolate ourselves, we create a different kind of pain—the anguish of loneliness and perpetual fear. Instead, we can determine to interpret our wounds as the fertile soil of growth instead of insurmountable barriers. Some people say that our greatest impact on others after we're forty comes as a direct result of the wounds we experience and resolve before that time. We have seen this principle in countless lives.

I (Paulus) live by this concept every day. My most effective ministry today was born from the most searing pain in my life. I know the devastation caused by chronic poverty because I lived on my own from the time I was six years old and carried water for families in exchange for a bowl of rice. I understand the fear people feel when they receive the diagnosis of cancer because I had that terrible disease and felt those overwhelming pangs of fear. I have compassion for those who face death because our family and students had to run for our lives from radical Muslim jihadists. I've lived in a refugee camp and watched my little girl Irene stop breathing when bombs exploded nearby. When people tell me about their hopes and dreams, I know; I have them too. And when people tell me about their deepest fears, I feel their emotions because I've been in similar places.

I had a lot of time to think while in the refugee camp. We had been serving the Lord, but the Muslims attacked us. I had tried to be a good father, but Irene was traumatized by the battle around us. I had tried to be a good husband, but all my efforts had led our family to this dead end in the filth of the camp. I had a choice: I could let the visible and emotional messages push me toward bitterness, or I could reinterpret the events and see them from an eternal point of view.

We chose to speak words of love and grace to those who hurt us, and eventually, almost all of them came back to apologize for treating us so badly. We didn't use those conversations to open old wounds. Like Joseph with his brothers, we had the opportunity to assure them that we had already forgiven them, and God used it to strengthen *us* as well, and equip us for a more effective ministry. They were amazed, and we were very glad.

Ready to Repack

To have the insight about what to throw away and what to keep on the journey, we need to be crystal clear about what the lepers have taught us so far:

- We're alive for a reason;

- We have a powerful drive to live in a way that has a profound impact on others;

- We have been given a lot of resources to invest in our work; and

- We have some friends who are our biggest cheerleaders as we find the courage to take each step.

As we respond to these first four steps—and probably not before—we realize we're carrying too much baggage. For some of us, we're not carrying a backpack of stuff; it's a dump truck load! We need clear purpose and motivation to give us the drive we need to make the hard decisions, we need the resources God has given us so we can make a difference in the lives of others, and we need our friends to help us wrestle the cumbersome baggage out of our lives.

When we're weighed down by the past's guilt, hurt, anger, and fear, we will almost certainly worry about the future. When we're consumed with the past and anxious about the future, we miss out on the joy of each day. Only when we let go of the hurt from the past can we pick up the resources of love, talents, and opportunities. We can then enjoy each day as we experience a deep sense of gratitude, peace, and contentment. We realize we can't control everything—but we have the incredible privilege of connecting with people to touch their hearts, and maybe change the trajectory of their lives.

When we repack, we make sure to keep the things that really matter. We let go of worry, but we hold on to our purpose. We let go of bitterness, but we make sure we keep honesty, grief, and forgiveness. We may need to let go of some people who are poisoning our hearts, but we continue to cherish those who are true friends.

Life is more than determination and discipline. To be sure, we encounter seasons in our lives when all we can do is take one more step. But even in the dark periods of life, we need to uncover sources of real joy. The love of God, the laughter of a child, the smile of a friend, the beauty of a sunrise . . . these and countless other wonders remind us of the things that make life worth living. Don't ever throw those things out of your backpack!

"The two most important days of your life are the day you are born and the day you find out why."
—**Mark Twain**

"The future belongs to those who believe in the beauty of their dreams."
—**Eleanor Roosevelt**

CHAPTER 7

SO WHAT? NOW WHAT?

The four individuals in ancient Israel who saved their nation were the least likely to become heroes. Just a few hours earlier they had only the slightest glimmer of hope they would even be alive to see the next sunrise. Their courage to take a risk was rewarded with fantastic riches, but they quickly realized they were meant for more than an expansive buffet and a new wardrobe—they were still alive for a much bigger purpose. The nation's future depended on them.

Don't miss the significance of this scene. They were outcasts among their own people. They had every reason to give up . . . or be selfish . . . or die in bitterness and self-pity. But they cared more for the people who had rejected them than they cared for their own comfort and reputations.

If those four men could make a difference, we can too. Our situations probably aren't as dire, our resources are greater, and our friends are more numerous than those lepers. We have far greater opportunities if we will only seize them.

Even You

If you've made it to this chapter, you must still have a desire for your life to count. You want to do something that matters.

You want to invest your time, your abilities, and your love to change the course of existence for people in need. You want to create something beautiful, give hope to the hopeless, rescue those who have fallen through the cracks of society, and bring a smile to sad faces.

Although many men and women are identified by name throughout the Bible, the four lepers are not. Why not? We believe it is because the writer wants us to see ourselves in these four men. We could be one of them . . . we *are* them! We have the same choice to rise above our circumstances, no matter how hopeless they seem, and do courageous and magnificent things that change the destiny of other people.

Everyone is included on the invitation list to lead a life of purpose. All of us can do something significant to touch the lives of others. When we talk about heroes, we often mention people whose talents are beyond our reach. Very few of us can play basketball like Lebron James, hit a golf ball like Tiger Woods, paint like Monet, sing like Mariah Carey, entertain like Michael Jackson, invest like Warren Buffett, or innovate like Steve Jobs. But, like the lepers, we can all look past our very real deficiencies and do something special. We don't have to be celebrities to make a difference.

Many people assume they don't have what it takes. They see only their limitations instead of their potential, and they become paralyzed. They have some faint dreams of doing something for others, but they assume they're disqualified because of something they lack, such as:

- Popularity among their peers;

- Exceptional talents in a particular area;

- A position of power;

- Economic prosperity;

- Family support;

- The right degree;

- Freedom from obligations to family and work;

- Physical stamina;

- Charisma;

- An easily identifiable platform to launch their efforts; or

- A prosperous and dynamic culture.

The lepers didn't have any of these things. In fact, their lives were seriously deficient in every area on this list. We tend to use the lack of such things as an excuse to sit on the sidelines and watch the world go by. People complain, "If I just had [plenty of money, enough time, my parents' support, some great ability to share, the 'right' personality, or any of a dozen other things], I could see myself doing something wonderful for others." That's bunk. People who use excuses need to look more closely at the lepers. They are our example of tenacious courage and a heart that cares more for others than personal comfort. If excuses didn't paralyze them, our excuses look pretty silly.

People call America "the land of opportunity" because Americans have easy access to resources. But Paulus has accomplished more with less in Indonesia than the vast majority of people do in America. We need to remember, "To whom much is given, much is required." That's not a guilt motivation but a desire to be good managers of all we have in our hands.

We have met some heroes in the same category as the lepers—exemplary men and women who have risen above their circumstances to make a difference:

- A businessman has earned the respect of his peers at work by his integrity and wisdom. He is rising in the company, but not by stepping on people on his way up. He genuinely cares for the people who work in his division . . . and they know it. He uses his platform to be a mentor to several young executives who benefit from his guidance.

- Another man realized he was always exhausted and preoccupied after work when he finally got home to his wife and three children. A friend challenged him to make his first hour at home the best hour of his day. That new vision of the positive influence he could have on his family revolutionized his perspective . . . and their relationships.

- A single mother has her hands full with all her responsibilities, yet she volunteers at her church to share with other young mothers the wisdom she has learned.

- A couple in Indonesia left a profitable business because their hearts were touched by the needs of orphans. They moved into Mercy Home, an orphanage, and are pouring their love into thirty children.

- A group of singles discovered the plight of young women who had been sold into sex slavery. They have devoted their time and energy to free the enslaved women in their city and help them find good jobs and hopeful futures.

- A physician worked hard for years and looked forward to retirement, but he realized he could do more with his life than play golf. He helped plant a church, and he donates much of his income to get the church off the ground. But his commitment is not just monetary. He began praying with and for each of his patients. Now he has a new reason to go to work each day.

- A couple nearing retirement was touched by the need for medical care in Africa. After investigating a number of organizations, they have invested a large portion of their income in one of them.

- A man who served in his state's senate led one of the most important committees in the past decade. Many who knew him realized he was a likely candidate for a run for the governor's seat. He thought about it long and hard because he had a very good chance to win, but he had a commitment to his wife and two children, one of whom is physically challenged. He told his supporters, "Thanks, but I have plenty to do here and now."

- A high school teacher was frustrated that two of his students were falling behind. They were bright, but they often failed to do their homework. He talked with each of them about their lack of progress, and he discovered their dads had both lost their jobs at a local factory. He decided to do two things: he called some local business leaders to set up job interviews for the men, and he volunteered to mentor the two students to help them catch up. The mentoring program he initiated has really expanded. Seven other teachers now join him to help students after school three days a week.

Too many of us spend time and money to insulate ourselves from the needs of people in our communities, and we aren't moved by news reports of wars, famine, and natural disasters. If we open our eyes and hearts, we will see plenty of needs around us and around the world. A broken heart is a sign that we're human. We can't repair every undesirable situation, but we can make a difference in one of them.

The Benefit of a Crisis

Human nature wants to avoid stress at all costs. When we encounter difficulties, we instinctively ask for relief, and we want it immediately! Our ultimate purposes, however, are much bigger than our comfort. God often uses crises to teach us life's most important lessons. If we pay attention, we can learn a lot.

Difficulties strip away the thin layers of self-protection and denial. They force us to be honest about our purpose, our motivations, how we use our resources, our most important relationships, and the baggage we carry. Heartaches and headaches remind us to ask the five questions again. We need to ask them often if we're going to stay sharp. Crises provide fertile ground to reconsider our answers and make any necessary corrections.

Hard times often trigger cycles of growth in our lives. We begin with a *promise*, then we face a *problem*, and we search for God's *provision*. The cycle is often evident in the lives of heroic figures, but we can usually find it in our own experiences, too. We have a vision to do something. We feel challenged, inspired, and energized to get going, yet after we begin we almost invariably encounter obstacles. Perhaps we are naïve and don't anticipate potential difficulties, or maybe we plan very well yet encounter setbacks that seem to come out of nowhere. Even our most trusted friends walk away, or an economic collapse shatters our best plans. At that moment, we face the potential death of our dream. We can either quit . . . or look to God for a solution. Quite often, God answers in a way that is totally unexpected. We might hope and pray for a particular answer, but he gives us something completely different. If we're not alert, we might miss it. But if we're paying attention, we will find that his answer is better than our original plans.

This pattern doesn't happen just once in a lifetime. It occurs over and over again. In fact, each cycle gets bigger and bolder: a more expansive vision, more daunting problems, and more surprising provisions. Each time, our faith is stretched a little more. We may want to quit or run away, but we remember: *I found the solution the last dozen times when this happened, and I'm sure I'll find one again.*

The most successful people aren't those who have no problems. They're the ones who don't quit when they encounter life's difficulties. They recognize the cycle of growth, so they aren't shocked when problems threaten to derail their plans. Instead, they learn, grow even stronger, trust, and reach even higher the next time.

If we view problems as the end of the world, we will fail to rise to the challenge, and we will miss the opportunity to grow. But if we realize problems are part of life—the classroom where we learn valuable lessons—we will embrace struggles instead of resenting them.

Your Script

All of us have a story to tell, and we are all still writing our stories. Some might shake their heads, "No, not me. My life is too dull." If that's what they think, they can rewrite the script. Others may complain, "It's too late. You don't know what terrible things I've done." Don't you understand? The very best stories, the ones that make us sit on the edge of our seats, are the tales of underdogs fighting against the odds and suffering setbacks, but finally coming out on top! Think of your favorite movies. None of them are about nice people doing bland things. They are filled with characters, risks, dangers, and opposition—just like your life is, or just like your life can be.

You can't possibly have less going for you than the four lepers. You can't have more hurdles to overcome than they did. Do you worry about your complexion? They had leprosy. Do you wonder about your job security? They were unemployable. Do you feel rejected? No one would even dare touch them. Do you have concerns about your future? They were stuck at the base of the city wall for the rest of their lives.

Yet they didn't let anything stop them from rewriting the story of their lives and completely changing the script.

In *Leading with a Limp*, Dan Allender encourages people to see the darker strands of their stories as essential to make them interesting. But analyzing our scripts takes courage. He wrote:

"Since you were there when your story happened, entering it would seem like the easiest thing in the world to do, but actually, nothing is more difficult. The reason is we only know—or let ourselves know—part of our story. We hold on either to what we wish to remember or to what serves us well to recall, and we flee from the parts of our story that most deeply expose and unnerve us. . . . If [a person] plunges into his own story, then he will understand better where he refuses to live with faith, hope, and love. He will better be able to name how he attempts to make truth serve his own idolatry rather than allowing the lies of his life to be exposed by the searing goodness of God. In the midst of this tension, we can live in the truest truth."

When the four lepers intuitively answered the five questions, some things *in* them and *about* them radically changed, but other things stayed the same. In their desperation, they took a risk to try the impossible and trust the improbable. When they found the food, clothing, and riches in the enemy camp, they also found a new sense of purpose—to live for a cause greater than themselves.

We might conclude, "For those guys, everything changed!" But it didn't. The events that happened to them that night and the next day were certainly dramatic, but the men were, in fact, still lepers. They were still outcasts who still had many of the same challenges they had faced since they contracted their disease. But now they had something no one could take away from them: the experience of a wonderful—even miraculous—turnaround in the trajectory of their lives. They were still lepers, but they had new hopes for the future, deeper connections with each other, and a dramatic experience they would remember the rest of their lives. They had a story to tell!

In the same way, our circumstances don't magically change when we find a new purpose. Living with a fresh, compelling sense of meaning doesn't mean our IQs will rise, we will hit the lottery, we will find the spouse of our dreams, a best friend will suddenly appear, the diagnosis will be reversed, the boss will suddenly become respectful and affirming, or we will get taller and better looking. The pursuit of purpose doesn't promise to make our lives easier, but it will ensure that every day will be a word, a sentence, or a chapter in our life's story—a story that we're sure really matters. It's what gets us up each day with renewed hope and courage to face every challenge.

The five questions of the lepers (and their responses) can help you take a long look at the story of your life. Take a look at them one more time, and as you do, consider the story you have written so far and the story you want to write from this point forward.

1) "Why am I still alive?"

2) "Why do I do what I do?"

3) "Why do I have what I have?"

4) "Who is going with me?"

5) "What am I carrying on the journey?"

An old saying reminds us, "When you write the story of your life, don't let anyone else hold the pen!" At this point in your life you may have allowed problematic relationships, attitudes, self-image, or any number of other issues to create writer's block, stalling the progress you hoped to make toward a happy ending. But from here on, it's up to you. It's entirely up to you. You may not even know what you want to write yet, but our guess is that you've read this book in order to take some big steps to figure it out.

As you think through the five questions, other questions are likely to spring to mind as you attempt to clarify your sense of purpose. For example:

- What makes my heart sing?

- What needs in the lives of people burden me?

- What can I see myself doing that will make a difference?

- What resources will I need in the future to accomplish my dreams?

- What risks can I expect to face?

- What rewards do I expect?

The answers to these and similar questions become the sentences, the paragraphs, and the chapters of your story. You will have plenty of drama in unexpected plot twists and sudden setbacks, so be ready for them. They're all part of the story, and in retrospect you will see those things are what make your story thrilling for you and interesting to others.

Overcoming Reluctance

As we near the end of the book, we hope you feel inspired and challenged, but those emotions are very likely mingled with confusion and fear. You want to make an impact, but you're not sure where to start. You long for your life to count, but you're afraid your friends will think you're insane.

Whenever you change directions and try something new, mixed feelings are inevitable—but don't let the fears crowd out the excitement. Don't assume you need to do something huge and dramatic. A few people may need to make a drastic change in the direction of their lives, but most of us just need to take the next step, no matter how small it may seem. God will put someone or a cause on your heart. Do what you can with what you already have in hand. Take one step, and see how God uses you. Then take the next step, and the next.

It's not enough to have a plan, even a carefully crafted plan. We have to act. We have to know we're alive, we have a purpose, we have resources in our hands, we're going with the right friends, and we can identify the things that hold us back. But it's not enough just to *know* these things. You need to take action, so do something now:

- Ask a coworker about her weekend. ✓ Juya

- Hug your spouse.

- Get on the floor and play with your ~~kids~~. *GRACIE* ✓

- Smile at someone you pass on the street.

- Give a hand to an elderly person who is trying to climb some steps.

- Speak words of kindness to someone who annoys you.

- Get in the slow line at the grocery store—on purpose—and ✓ tell the frazzled cashier how much you appreciate her service. *BETHANY*

- Write a note to a lonely relative.

- Call a friend who could use some encouragement.

- Stop to talk to a neighbor instead of rushing inside when you get home. ✓ *LAURIE*

- Turn off the computer and television so you can have some time to think or read.

When we imagine living a life of significance, we usually think of starting large organizations, giving millions of dollars, or sacrificing everything for a cause. Those are rare instances, indeed. For most people, the story of significance is told in the faces of those who receive our tokens of love, attention, and kindness.

The reason the lepers are significant is not because they got rich in the enemy camp. The power of their story is that they made a single, brave, compassionate decision that saved a city. Men and women, boys and girls, didn't starve to death. They all gained a future because of one selfless decision.

Your story of purpose and investment may never be told in the pages of your local newspaper, but it will certainly be told in the hearts and lives of the people who become convinced that you love them. How do they know? Because you do the little things that make a huge difference. It may only be telling them some good news, but that's enough to change their day, and perhaps, the rest of their lives.

If you already had a clear, compelling sense of purpose when you picked up this book, we hope you feel wonderfully affirmed. Keep going! If the story of the four lepers has helped you realize you've been headed in the wrong direction, you can make a radical redirection. If you weren't sure what your purpose was when you opened the first page, we hope the story of the lepers has helped to clarify your thinking and your direction in life. Many of us have an idea of our purpose, but we need to continually make midcourse corrections to our direction, our motives, our resources, our friends, and our baggage.

It's never too late. You walk past people every day who desperately need you to stop and care for them. No excuses . . . no delays. Do something now. Don't waste your life. Make a difference.

> "Courage is being scared to death . . . and saddling up anyway."
> —*John Wayne*

"You're a leader. It's your job to keep your passion hot.
Do whatever you have to do, read whatever you have
to read, go wherever you have to go to stay fired up.
And don't apologize to anybody."
—**Bill Hybels**

ENDNOTES

p 26.   This is an adaptation, with some creativity and imagination, of the story in 2 Kings 6:24–7:20.

p 37.   Po Bronson and Ashley Merryman, "The Creativity Crisis," Newsweek, July 10, 2010.

p 39.   Tony Barnhart, "Bowden celebrates new book, new life," *College Football,* August 24, 2010, blogs. ajc.com/barnhart-college-football/2010/08/24/ bobby-bowden-celebrates-new-book-new-life/?cp=2

p 48.   And now I have a word . . . James 4:13-14 (*The Message*).

p 51.   Greater love has no one . . . John 15:13

p 51.   The Hebrew term *hebel,* translated *vanity* or *vain,* refers concrete-ly to a "mist," "vapor," or "mere breath." (See Ecclesiastes 1:2, ESV.)

p 53.   "Stress Is the New Fat (and Busy Is the New Fine)," Jonathan Fields, *Psychology Today*, August 17, 2012, www. psychologytoday.com/blog/awake-the-wheel/201208/ stress-is-the-new-fat-and-busy-is-the-new-fine

p 53.   "Variation in suicide occurrence," Maldonado and Kraus, www.ncbi.nlm.nih.gov/pubmed/1887454. "Heart Attack Risk Factors Rise on Mondays," Dr. Stephen Sinatra, www.drsinatra.com/ heart-attack-risk-factors-rise-on-mondays

p 55.   John Ortberg, *God Is Closer Than You Think* (Grand Rapids: Zondervan, 2005), p. 74.

p 59. "Maslow's Hierarchy of Needs," Saul McLeod, *Simply Psychology*, 2014, www.simplypsychology.org/maslow.html

p 60. C.S. Lewis, *Mere Christianity* (New York: HarperCollins, 1952), 122.

p 61. C. S. Lewis, *Surprised by Joy* (New York: Harcourt, Brace, Jovanovich, 1966), p. 161.

p 61. Henri Nouwen, *The Inner Voice of Love* (New York: Doubleday, 1998), p. 70.

p 64. "How does the reward center in the brain work?" Curiosity.com, curiosity.discovery.com/question/reward-center-in-brain-work

p 69. For a more detailed description of the intersection of affinity, ability, and opportunity, consult Kevin's previous book, *8 Essential Exchanges*, pp. 135–138

p 70. This is my beloved Son . . . Matthew 3:16.

p 71. The story about Ian Pitt-Watson and his daughter, Rosemary, by Philip Yancey, *Reaching for the Invisible God* (Grand Rapids: Zondervan, 2000), p. 165.

p 74. "The Olympic Legacy," Jerry Grillo, *Georgia Trend*, August 2006, www.georgiatrend.com/August-2006/The-Olympic-Legacy/

p 81. Kyle Williams is very happy for us to tell his story in our book.

p 82. *Increase my standard of giving* . . . Cited in *The Treasure Principle: Discovering the Secret of Joyful Giving* by Randy Alcorn (New York: Waterbrook Multnomah, 2001).

p 83.   One of the great designs . . . Cited at jan.ucc.nau.edu/~jsa3/
hum355/readings/ellul.htm

p 84.   Dale Carnegie, *The 5 Essential People Skills* (New York: Simon &
Schuster, 2009), Chapter 7.

p 99.   "Malcolm Gladwell on Rugged Individualism and the Myth
of American Success," John Zahl, February 18, 2009, www.mbird.
com/2009/02/malcolm-gladwell-on-debunking-rugged/

p 100. Rejoice with those who rejoice . . . Romans 12:15.

p 105. Jim Collins, *Good to Great*, (New York: HarperCollins, 2001), 62.

p 111. "Find Out Who Your Friends Are" (from the Tracy Lawrence
album, *For the Love*. Writers: Casey Beathard and Edward Monroe Hill.
© Sony/ATV Acuff Rose Music, Sagrabeaux Songs, Universal Music).

p 123. Lewis Smedes, *The Art of Forgiving: When You Need to Forgive
and Don't Know How* (New York: Ballantine Books, 1996), p. 171.

p 127. "Nelson Mandela: Tributes in Quotes," bio., cited at www.
biography.com/news/nelson-mandela-tributes-in-quotes

p 130. Do not fear . . . Genesis 50:19-21 (The Message). And to review
the entire story of Joseph's life with its many intriguing details, see
Genesis chapters 37 and 39–50.

p 138. To whom much is given . . . Luke 12:48.

p 143. Dan Allender, *Leading with a Limp* (Colorado Springs:
Waterbrook Press, 2006), p. 161.

THINK ABOUT IT . . .

As you finish reading each chapter, take time to answer the questions on the following pages that help you consider and apply the principles described in the chapter. This isn't a speed drill. Take your time, be honest, and reflect on the most important questions you'll ever consider. We've left a little room for you to write. If you need more space, use a notebook to record your reflections.

1. Describe the sense of desperation the four lepers experienced as the story began.

2. After they got to the Syrian camp, the men ate and grabbed as much stuff as they could hide. What are some possible motives that could have prompted them to look beyond their own wants to care for the starving people back in the city? Which of these seem noble and good? Which seem less than honorable?

3. Review the five questions. Why do you think they are "a package" so that all of them need to be answered? What if some aren't addressed?

4. Do you agree or disagree that the best consultants are those who ask the best questions, not those who give all the right answers? Explain your answer.

5. Read Jeremiah 29:11. What would it mean for you to have a God-inspired sense of purpose?

6. What do you hope to get from this book? What are your fears or doubts that have come into your mind as you read this chapter?

7. On a scale of 0 (not at all) to 10 (totally), how sure are you that God has a specially designed purpose for your life? How does your answer to this question affect your sense of adventure and your willingness to pursue your dreams?

1. At what point do you think the four lepers actually realized they *weren't* going to die? How would you have responded if you were one of them at that moment?

2. Many people don't want to think about their mortality, but some are obsessed with death. What's a healthy way to grasp the significance of our mortality?

3. Why do you think "busy" is the new "fine"? What do we hope our busyness earns for us in the eyes of others?

4. Do you agree or disagree that true purpose is always bigger than our success, pleasure, and approval? Whom do you know who has achieved a measure of these things and still feels empty?

5. Read Luke 12:13-21. What was the point of Jesus' parable? Does it inspire you or terrify you? How can the message of his story help you live with a new, vibrant sense of purpose?

6. How does the love of Christ give us the security we need so we can look beyond ourselves and genuinely care for others?

7. How would you answer the question: "Why am I still alive?"

CHAPTER 3

MOTIVATION: "WHY DO I DO WHAT I DO?"

1. Describe how and why the lepers' motivations changed.

2. What are some evidences of the ways comparison affects our thoughts, our desires, our relationships, and our purpose?

3. What are some ways each of these motivate you?

- Survival:

- Approval:

- Fun:

- Hidden drives:

- Calling:

4. How would you explain the grace of God to a friend?

5. What would it mean for you to let God's grace sink deep into your heart and change you from the inside out?

6. Read Ephesians 4:1-3. What does it mean to "walk in a manner worthy of the calling to which you have been called"?

7. Who are some people you know, even two or three, who get up every day with a sense of God's calling and can't wait to make a difference in the lives of others?

8. How would you answer the question, "Why do I do what I do?"

1. What do you think may have prompted at least one of the lepers to realize he (and they) were "doing wrong" if they didn't let the city know what they had found in the Syrian camp?

2. What is the meaning of money to you? Explain your answer.

3. Describe the ways modern advertising tries to create an image of an "ideal" life . . . and promises to deliver it. What commercials stand out as the most alluring? What are the obvious promises of the products or services (like whiter teeth)? What are the hidden and more seductive promises (like being popular)?

4. Why do you think there are no happy guilty people or happy stingy people?

5. In what way is generosity always an overflow for a person who has been the recipient of radical generosity?

6. What are some things you can do today to be generous to others?

7. Read the parable in Luke 12:13–21. What did the man demand of Jesus? What was Jesus' reply? Does his warning sound harsh or pretty accurate? Explain your answer.

8. How would you answer the question: "Why do I have what I have?"

CHAPTER 5

FRIENDS: "WHO IS GOING WITH ME?"

1. Why do you think the lepers' friendship mattered so much—
    to them and eventually to the people in the city? Why did they
    need each other?

2. Do you agree or disagree with the statement: "The quality of
    your friendships determines the quality of your life"? Explain
    your answer.

3. Who are your peers? Who are mentors who have shaped
    your life? Who are you pouring your life into? How would
    you evaluate the current condition of these three spheres of
    relationships?

4. Which of your friends are calling you to your highest and best, and which ones bring out your lowest and least?

5. What are the most difficult relationships of your life? What lessons did you (or could you) learn from those painful experiences? Would you consider thanking those people for playing a role in your growth?

6. How can you know when to invest time, attention, love, and truth in a person who is annoying or difficult? And when is it time for the season to end? Is there anything in between?

7. Describe how Jesus embodied grace and truth in every relationship: with his closest followers, with misfits and outcasts, and with those who opposed him.

8. How would you answer the question: "Who is going with me?"

CHAPTER 6

BAGGAGE: "WHAT AM I CARRYING ON THE JOURNEY?"

1. Have you ever seen anyone who had to repack a suitcase at the airport? What was his or her attitude? How did it affect the person at that moment and for the rest of the trip?

2. Why is it essential to define our destination before we can know what to throw away and what to keep?

3. Why do anger, resentment, self-pity, fear, and other "bad baggage" often feel so comfortable and right? What does it cost to keep them? What does it cost to replace them with love, joy, and purpose? (We pay a price either way.)

4. Look at Ephesians 4:31–32. What is the connection between our *experience* of Christ's forgiveness and our capacity and motivation to *express* forgiveness to those who have hurt us?

5. Would you agree or disagree that the most important lessons we learn are usually from our most painful experiences? Explain your answer.

6. What do you need to do in the repack zone? Who is a trusted friend who can help you?

7. What difference will it make for you to resolve the pain of the past and replace the worry about the future with a new sense of hope?

8. How would you answer the question: "What am I carrying on the journey?"

CHAPTER 7

SO WHAT? NOW WHAT?

1. What factors make people feel disqualified from making an impact on others? Which of these have hindered *your* quest for purpose? How does the grace of God transform your identity and change you from the inside out?

2. Do you think it's easier to make a difference in America or in Indonesia (or in another country)? Explain why.

3. What are some ways people insulate themselves from the needs of others and become anesthetized to the news of tragedies around the world?

4. Describe the cycle of growth. How have you seen it work in the lives of people who are making a difference? How have you seen it work in your life?

5. It's normal to have a sense of reluctance to change direction and try something new. How would you describe your mixed feelings of inspiration and fear? Which one is stronger right now?

6. What are three "next things" that you can do today?

7. As you think back through the entire book, what are the most important lessons you've learned from the four lepers?

8. What will you do with the lessons you've learned? How will they lead to a life of significance?

LEADING A GROUP OR CLASS USING
THE LEPERS' LESSONS

This book is designed for individual study, small groups, and classes. The best way to absorb and apply the principles is for each person to individually study and answer the questions for each chapter at the end of the book, then discuss them in either a class or a group environment. The interaction stimulates insights and applications.

Order enough copies of the book for each person to have a copy. For couples, encourage both to have their own book so they can record their individual reflections.

A recommended schedule for a small group or class might be:

Week 1

Introduce the material. As a group leader, tell your story of finding and fulfilling God's purpose, share your hopes for the group, and provide books for each person. Encourage people to read the assigned chapter each week and answer the questions. For the next week, ask them to read the Introduction and the first chapter.

Weeks 2–8

Each week, introduce the topic for the week and share a story of how God has used the principles in your life. In small groups, lead people through a discussion of the questions at the end of the chapter. In classes, teach the principles in each chapter, use personal illustrations, and invite discussion.

Personalize Each Lesson

Don't feel pressured to cover every question in your group discussions. Pick out three or four that had the biggest impact on you, and focus on those, or ask people in the group to share their responses to the questions that meant the most to them that week.

Make sure to personalize the principles and applications. At least once in each group meeting, add your own story to illustrate a particular point.

If you look at a passage from the Bible, make the Scriptures come alive. Far too often we read the Bible like it's a phone book, with little or no emotion. Paint a vivid picture for people. Provide insights about the context of people's encounters with God, and help those in your class or group sense the emotions of specific people in each scene.

Focus on Application

The reflection questions and your encouragement for group members to be authentic will help your group take important steps to apply the principles they're learning. Share how you are applying the principles in particular chapters each week, and encourage them to take steps of growth, too.

Three Types of Questions

If you have led groups for a few years, you already understand the importance of using open questions to stimulate discussion. Three types of questions are *limiting, leading,* and *open.* Many of the questions at the end of each lesson are open questions.

Limiting questions focus on an obvious answer, such as, "What does Jesus call himself in John 10:11?" They don't stimulate reflection or discussion. If you want to use questions like these, follow them with thought-provoking, open questions.

Leading questions require the listener to guess what the leader has in mind, such as, "Why did Jesus use the metaphor of a shepherd in John 10?" (He was probably alluding to a passage in Ezekiel, but many people don't know that.) The teacher who asks a leading question has a definite answer in mind. Instead of asking this kind of question, you should just teach the point and perhaps ask an open question about the point you have made.

Open questions usually don't have right or wrong answers. They stimulate thinking, and they are far less threatening because the person answering doesn't risk ridicule for being wrong. These questions often begin with "Why do you think . . .?" or "What are some reasons that . . .?" or "How would you have felt in that situation?"

Preparation

As you prepare to teach this material in a group or class, consider these steps:

1. Carefully and thoughtfully read the book. Make notes, highlight key sections, quotes, or stories, and complete the reflection section at the end of each chapter. This will familiarize you with the entire scope of the content.

2. As you prepare for each week's class or group, read the corresponding chapter again and make additional notes.

3. Tailor the amount of content to the time allotted. You may not have time to cover all the questions, so pick the ones that are most pertinent.

4. Add your own stories to personalize the message and add impact.

5. Before and during your preparation, ask God to give you wisdom, clarity, and power. Trust him to use your group to change people's lives.

6. Most people will get far more out of the group if they read the chapter and complete the reflection each week. Order books before the group or class begins or after the first week.

Kevin is the author of *8 Essential Exchanges*, a book that helps people clarify their most important decisions in life. Kevin Paul Scott has traveled to six continents and spoken to leaders from more than 100 countries. Kevin co-founded both ADDO Worldwide and the ADDO Institute. The ADDO Institute received the Governor's International Award for "New Company of the Year" in the state of Georgia. The Institute works specifically in the areas of global leadership, student leadership and thought leadership.

Prior to founding ADDO, Kevin's background included non-profit charitable work, business ventures, and politics. After

graduating from the University of Georgia, Kevin served on a presidential campaign team and then worked as a representative for a United States Congressman.

Kevin was named one of the "Power 30 Under 30" for his work in expanding the marketing efforts nationwide as the Communicator in Chief for a global company. In consecutive years, Kevin was named to the "40 under 40" lists for *Georgia Trend* and then the *Atlanta Business Chronicle*.

For his leadership and business acumen, Kevin has been featured on Fox Business, CNBC and in numerous publications, including The *New York Times, Washington Post, Los Angeles Times, Atlanta Journal Constitution, Detroit Free Press, The Economist* and others.

For fun, Kevin has been cage diving with Great White Sharks in South Africa, trekked Mountain Gorillas in Uganda, and ridden a llama in Colombia. However, he most enjoys being at home to cheer on the Atlanta Braves and Georgia Bulldogs. Kevin was raised in Kennesaw, Georgia, and is active in his local church. Known for his grassroots appeal and southern charm, Kevin speaks extensively at businesses, universities and within the faith community.

ADDO Worldwide

ADDO is a brand + experience consultancy. ADDO helps businesses and brands ideate and activate initiatives to enhance leadership and social impact. ADDO creates ways for companies to maximize "doing business" while "doing good" to deliver tangible, sustainable and measurable engagement with customers and their communities.

ADDO Worldwide consults on strategic business initiatives, communication strategies, and effective employee engagement. In partnership with Chick-fil-A, ADDO Worldwide has created a high school leadership program: Chick-fil-A Leader Academy. The innovative program teaches project-based leadership and emphasizes "impact through action."

ADDO Institute

ADDO Institute is a registered $501(c)(3)$ not-for-profit organization that engages individuals of all ages through leadership development and cultural travel.

The ADDO Institute received the Governor's International Award for "New Company of the Year" in the State of Georgia.

For more information, go to www.addo.is

ABOUT PAULUS WIRATNO

Paulus Wiratno is the founder of discipleMaker International, an organization that is impacting lives throughout Indonesia. dMaker has three branches of ministry: Mercy Indonesia, Radio Dian Mandiri, and a church planting school.

Paulus and his wife Marliesye live in Denpasar, Bali. They have three children: Debora, Irene, and Timothy.

Mercy Indonesia

dMaker currently has twelve orphanages on islands throughout Indonesia.

The mission of Mercy Indonesia is to restore the lives of children and teenagers who have been orphaned through natural

disasters, religious wars or that have been rescued from sex slavery. They partner with churches, corporations, and individuals who have a passion to help needy people.

Mercy Indonesia provides emotional care, spiritual guidance, education, and the basics to meet physical needs. The focus is show the love of Jesus Christ and restore dignity to those who are hurting most.

Radio Dian Mandiri (which means "Independent Light")

Radio is a great vehicle for sowing seeds of the gospel, opening doors, and preparing the hearts of thousands of people to understand and experience the grace of Jesus Christ. Through broadcasts on 44 stations, Muslims, Hindus, and Christians hear practical messages about how they can make their family lives better. In addition to the preaching of God's word, listeners hear testimonies, uplifting worship, and other programs that are aired daily.

In Indonesia, radio is a powerful tool to reach people and influence their perspectives on the most important issues in their lives. The programs on Radio Dian Mandiri challenge faulty perceptions and invite people to embrace God's truth. Through radio, lives are being transformed.

One of the goals of this ministry is to raise money to distribute 50,000 solar-powered radios that are pre-tuned to the local Radio Dian Mandiri stations. This technology is especially effective in remote areas that lack access to electricity. The radios cost only $18 each.

Church Planting School

Indonesia has the fourth largest population of any country in the world. In 2011, the population was 241 million, 85 percent of whom are Muslims. The island nation contains hundreds of unique

cultures, tribes, and languages. The task of reaching them with the gospel of Jesus Christ requires creativity, courage, and tenacity.

dMaker has established a one-year training curriculum to equip people to plant new churches. In the next decade, dMaker hopes to plant a church in every city, town, and village in Indonesia. More immediately, the goal is to release at least 250 church planters each year. Between 2000 and 2012, 1361 people have graduated from our church planting schools, and 1553 new churches have been planted.

Most of our church planters are bi-vocational. The challenge for these individuals is to find enough financial support so they can focus their time and energy on evangelism, discipleship, and caring for the needy. The leaders don't need much. Only $125 a month will sponsor a church planter and release him to be fully engaged in his calling.

For more information about these three branches of disciple-Maker ministries, go to www.imercy.org

ACKNOWLEDGEMENTS

From Kevin ...

First and foremost, I'm thankful for Christ. I know that true meaning in life is found in the security of His love and the life-changing purpose He has for all of us.

This book would simply not have happened without the help and encouragement of many people. In particular, I want to thank ...

... Pat Springle, who worked tirelessly to help put the thoughts for this book into words. In addition to being an incredible writer and publisher, he has become a great friend.

... Garrett Gravesen, who believed in this dream, not just with affirming words but also with generous actions.

... My parents, Jeff and Lynne, for all of their sacrifices and raising me in a godly home.

... And the rest of my family, including my sister Whitney, brother-in-law Jon, and Uncle Mark. I greatly appreciate your support and encouragement.

I would like to thank the ADDO team for helping inspire people today to make impact tomorrow: Laura Engelbrecht, Todd Williams, Elizabeth Jay, and the others who are on the journey with us.

I am also very grateful to the individuals who have been encouragers along the way: Laura Burch, Vince and Barbara Dooley, Deanna Dooley, John Hull, Melissa McEachern, Billy Boughey, and John Hightower.

Thank you to David Johnson and the team at Strategic Vision for providing a platform to reach more people.

And thanks to many wonderful people at Chick-fil-A, including David Salyers, L.J. Yankowsky, John Mattioli, Jessica Purser, John Shackelford, Rodney Bullard, Melonie Flavin, Mark Miller and the Cathy family. I am grateful for your partnership to impact students across America.

Finally, thanks to Paulus for taking this journey with me. I believe in you and I'm grateful for your heart for others.

From Paulus ...

I am thankful for many pastors—especially Mike Murphy, Rod Plummer, Jack Hanes and Rich Witmer—who have given me invaluable encouragement in times of hardship. These men have proven that true friendship is the real wealth in life.

Thanks to my friends Kyle Williams, Devon and Cindy Dickinson, and Craig Muller, who have inspired my family and me and have shown me true generosity.

I am also grateful to Kevin Scott, Pat Springle, and Garrett Gravesen, without whom this book would have never been published.

TO ORDER MORE COPIES

For more information or to order copies of this book, go to
www.KevinPaulScott.com

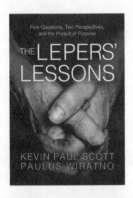

The Lepers' Lessons is also available
on Amazon.com, Kindle, Nook
and iBooks.

Also available from Kevin Paul
Scott, *8 Essential Exchanges: What
You Have to Give Up to Go Up*